Slow Cooker

100 mouth-watering recipes • Clear and easy-to-follow ingredients lists • Step-by-step instructions

D1492942

This edition published in 2013
LOVE FOOD is an imprint of Parragon Books Ltd

Parragon
Chartist House
15–17 Trim Street
Bath, BA1 1HA, UK

www.parragon.com/lovefood

ISBN: 978-1-78186-074-8

Printed in China

Produced by Ivy Contract
Cover and additional internal photography by Mike Cooper
Cover and additional home economy and food styling by Lincoln Jefferson
New recipes written by Christine France

Notes for the Reader

This book uses both metric and imperial measurements. Follow the same units of measurement throughout; do not mix metric and imperial. All spoon measurements are level: teaspoons are assumed to be 5 ml, and tablespoons are assumed to be 15 ml. Unless otherwise stated, milk is assumed to be full fat, eggs and individual vegetables are medium, and pepper is freshly ground black pepper.

The times given are an approximate guide only. Preparation times differ according to the techniques used by different people and the cooking times may also vary from those given. Optional ingredients, variations or serving suggestions have not been included in the calculations.

Recipes using raw or very lightly cooked eggs should be avoided by infants, the elderly, pregnant women, convalescents and anyone suffering from an illness. Pregnant and breastfeeding women are advised to avoid eating peanuts and peanut products. Sufferers from nut allergies should be aware that some of the ready-made ingredients used in the recipes in this book may contain nuts. Always check the packaging before use.

Vegetarians should be aware that some of the ready-made ingredients used in the recipes in this book may contain animal products. Always check the packaging before use.

For front cover recipe, please see page 90.

Slow Cooker

introduction

For busy people, a slow cooker can provide that most elusive culinary combination: healthy home-cooked food *and* convenience. With minimum effort, you can serve up a meal that is tender and flavoursome whilst saving time and money – what could be better? Just put the ingredients into the slow cooker in the morning, switch it on and leave it to cook whilst you go to work and get on with your life. As the slow cooker cooks at a very low temperature, cooking times are quite flexible – you needn't worry about your meal burning if you are a little late, and even an amateur cook can rustle up a spectacular dish.

For the health conscious, slow cooking doesn't require much oil, and the nutrients in vegetables stay in the pot rather than being lost through boiling and draining. Slow cooking makes cheaper, tougher cuts of meat deliciously tender, saving you money on your shopping, and because a slow cooker only uses as much electricity as a lightbulb it will cut down your electricity bill too! All kinds of dishes can be prepared, and because everything is cooked in one pot there is less washing-up to do afterwards.

This book will introduce you to the range of sumptuous meals that you can prepare in your slow cooker, from warming winter casseroles, low-fat vegetable soups and spicy curries to indulgent desserts. There are dishes to suit every occasion and taste with a mouth-watering selection of meals that are suitable for all the family. All it needs is a little planning and preparation in advance so you can be assured that the perfect meal will be waiting for you when you return at the end of the day.

All the recipes featured in this book will fit into a 4.5 litre capacity slow cooker. Models vary slightly from one manufacturer to another, so make sure you check the instructions for your particular slow cooker, however the basics apply to all models. So turn the page, choose a recipe for a simple starter or a magnificent main course, and get ready to save money, eat healthily, and rediscover time just for you.

to start

chicken noodle soup

ingredients

serves 4

1 onion, diced
2 celery sticks, diced
2 carrots, diced
1 kg/2 lb 4 oz oven-ready chicken
700 ml/1¼ pints hot chicken stock
115 g/4 oz dried egg tagliatelle
2 tbsp chopped fresh dill, plus
    extra for serving
salt and pepper

method

1 Preheat the slow cooker, if necessary, or according to the manufacturer's instructions.

2 Place the onion, celery and carrots in the slow cooker. Season the chicken all over with salt and pepper and place on top. Pour the stock over. Cover and cook on low for 5 hours.

3 Carefully lift out the chicken and remove the meat from the carcass, discarding the bones and skin. Cut the meat into bite-sized pieces.

4 Skim the excess fat from the juices, then return the chicken to the slow cooker. Turn the setting to high.

5 Bring a large saucepan of lightly salted water to the boil. Add the tagliatelle, return to the boil and cook for 5 minutes. Drain well.

6 Stir the tagliatelle and dill into the pot, cover and cook on high for a further 20 minutes. Serve immediately, in wide bowls, sprinkled with dill.

new england clam chowder

ingredients

serves 4

25 g/1 oz butter
1 onion, finely chopped
2 potatoes, peeled and cut
     into cubes
1 large carrot, diced
400 ml/14 fl oz fish stock or water
280 g/10 oz canned clams, drained
250 ml/9 fl oz double cream
salt and pepper
chopped fresh parsley, to garnish
fresh crusty bread, to serve

method

1 Preheat the slow cooker, if necessary, or according to the manufacturer's instructions.

2 Melt the butter in a frying pan, add the onion and fry over a medium heat for 4–5 minutes, stirring, until the onion is golden.

3 Transfer the onion to the slow cooker with the potatoes, carrot, stock and salt and pepper. Cover and cook on high for 3 hours.

4 Add the clams and the cream to the slow cooker and stir to mix evenly. Cover and cook for a further 1 hour.

5 Adjust the seasoning to taste then sprinkle with parsley and serve with crusty bread.

carrot & coriander soup

ingredients

serves 6

1 tbsp butter
1½ tbsp sunflower oil
1 Spanish onion, finely chopped
500 g/1 lb 2 oz carrots, diced
1-cm/½-inch piece fresh ginger,
    finely chopped
2 tsp ground coriander
1 tsp plain flour
1.2 litres/2 pints vegetable stock
150 ml/5 fl oz soured cream
2 tbsp chopped fresh coriander
salt and pepper
croûtons, to serve

method

1 Preheat the slow cooker, if necessary, or according to the manufacturer's instructions.

2 Melt the butter with the oil in a saucepan. Add the onion, carrots and ginger, cover and cook over a low heat, stirring occasionally, for 8 minutes, until softened and just beginning to colour.

3 Sprinkle over the ground coriander and flour and cook, stirring constantly, for 1 minute. Gradually stir in the stock, a little at a time, and bring to the boil, stirring constantly. Season to taste with salt and pepper.

4 Transfer the mixture to the slow cooker, cover and cook on low for 4–5 hours. Ladle the soup into a food processor or blender, in batches if necessary, and process until smooth. Return the soup to the slow cooker and stir in the soured cream. Cover and cook on low for a further 15–20 minutes, until heated through.

5 Ladle the soup into warmed soup bowls, garnish with the chopped coriander and sprinkle with croûtons. Serve immediately.

tomato & lentil soup

ingredients

serves 4

2 tbsp sunflower oil
1 onion, chopped
1 garlic clove, finely chopped
2 celery sticks, chopped
2 carrots, chopped
1 tsp ground cumin
1 tsp ground coriander
175 g/6 oz red or yellow lentils
1 tbsp tomato purée
1.2 litres/2 pints vegetable stock
400 g/14 oz canned
    chopped tomatoes
1 bay leaf
salt and pepper
crème fraîche and toasted crusty
    bread, to serve

method

1 Preheat the slow cooker, if necessary, or according to the manufacturer's instructions.

2 Heat the oil in a saucepan. Add the onion and garlic and cook over a low heat, stirring occasionally, for 5 minutes, until softened. Stir in the celery and carrots and cook, stirring occasionally, for a further 4 minutes. Stir in the ground cumin and coriander and cook, stirring, for 1 minute, then add the lentils.

3 Mix the tomato purée with a little of the stock in a small bowl and add to the pan with the remaining stock, the tomatoes and bay leaf. Bring to the boil, then transfer to the slow cooker. Stir well, cover and cook on low for 3½–4 hours.

4 Remove and discard the bay leaf. Transfer the soup to a food processor or blender and process until smooth. Season to taste with salt and pepper. Ladle into warmed soup bowls, top each with a swirl of crème fraîche and serve immediately with toasted crusty bread.

greek bean & vegetable soup

ingredients

serves 4–6

500 g/1 lb 2 oz dried haricot
   beans, soaked in water
   overnight, or for at least
   5 hours
2 onions, finely chopped
2 garlic cloves, finely chopped
2 potatoes, chopped
2 carrots, chopped
2 tomatoes, peeled and chopped
2 celery sticks, chopped
4 tbsp extra virgin olive oil
1 bay leaf
salt and pepper
12 black olives, stoned and
   halved and 2 tbsp chopped
   fresh chives, to serve

method

1 Preheat the slow cooker, if necessary, or according
   to the manufacturer's instructions.

2 Drain and rinse the beans, place in a saucepan, cover
   with fresh cold water, and bring to the boil. Boil rapidly
   for at least 10 minutes, then remove from the heat,
   drain and rinse again. Place them in the slow cooker
   and add the onions, garlic, potatoes, carrots, tomatoes,
   celery, olive oil and bay leaf.

3 Pour in 2 litres/3½ pints boiling water, making sure
   that all the ingredients are fully submerged. Cover and
   cook on low for 12 hours until the beans are tender.

4 Remove and discard the bay leaf. Season the soup to
   taste with salt and pepper and stir in the olives and
   chives. Ladle into warmed soup bowls or large mugs
   and serve.

cock-a-leekie soup

ingredients

serves 6–8

12 prunes, stoned, or
      12 ready-to-eat prunes
4 chicken portions
450 g/1 lb leeks, sliced
1.4 litres/2½ pints hot chicken
      or beef stock
1 bouquet garni
salt and pepper

method

1 Preheat the slow cooker, if necessary, or according to the manufacturer's instructions.

2 If using ordinary prunes, place them in a bowl and add cold water to cover. Set aside to soak while the soup is cooking.

3 Place the chicken portions and leeks in the slow cooker. Pour in the stock and add the bouquet garni. Cover and cook on low for 7 hours.

4 If you are going to serve the chicken in the soup, remove it from the cooker with a slotted spoon and cut the meat off the bones. Cut it into bite-sized pieces and return it to the cooker. Otherwise, leave the chicken portions in the slow cooker.

5 Drain the prunes, if necessary. Add the prunes to the soup and season to taste with salt and pepper. Re-cover and cook on high for 30 minutes.

6 Remove and discard the bouquet garni. Either ladle the soup, including the cut-up chicken, into warmed bowls or remove the chicken portions and keep warm for the main course, then ladle the broth into warmed bowls. Serve immediately.

bacon & lentil soup

ingredients

serves 6

450 g/1 lb thick, rindless smoked
    bacon rashers, diced
1 onion, chopped
2 carrots, sliced
2 celery sticks, chopped
1 turnip, chopped
1 large potato, chopped
85 g/3 oz green lentils
1 bouquet garni
1 litre/1¾ pints chicken
    stock or water
salt and pepper

method

1 Preheat the slow cooker, if necessary, or according
    to the manufacturer's instructions.

2 Heat a large, heavy-based saucepan. Add the bacon
    and cook over a low heat, stirring frequently, for
    4–5 minutes, until the fat runs. Add the onion, carrots,
    celery, turnip and potato and cook, stirring frequently,
    for 5 minutes.

3 Add the lentils and bouquet garni and pour in the
    stock. Bring to the boil, then transfer the mixture to
    the slow cooker. Cover and cook on low for 8–9 hours,
    or until the lentils are tender.

4 Remove and discard the bouquet garni and season the
    soup to taste with pepper and salt, if necessary. Ladle
    into warmed soup bowls and serve.

tex-mex bean dip

ingredients

serves 6

2 tbsp sunflower oil
1 onion, finely chopped
2 garlic cloves, finely chopped
2–3 fresh green chillies,
    deseeded and finely chopped
400 g/14 oz canned refried beans
    or red kidney beans
2 tbsp chilli sauce or taco sauce
6 tbsp hot vegetable stock
115 g/4 oz grated Cheddar cheese
salt and pepper
1 fresh red chilli, deseeded and
    shredded, to garnish
tortilla chips, to serve

method

1 Preheat the slow cooker, if necessary, or according to the manufacturer's instructions.

2 Heat the oil in a large, heavy-based frying pan. Add the onion, garlic and chillies and cook, stirring occasionally, over a low heat for 5 minutes until the onion is soft and translucent. Transfer to the slow cooker.

3 Add the refried beans to the slow cooker. If using red kidney beans, drain well and rinse under cold running water. Reserve 2 tablespoons of the beans and mash the remainder coarsely with a potato masher. Add all the beans to the slow cooker.

4 Add the sauce, hot stock and grated cheese, season with salt and pepper and stir well. Cover and cook on low for 2 hours.

5 Transfer the dip to a serving bowl, garnish with shredded red chilli and serve warm with tortilla chips on the side.

sweet & sour chicken wings

ingredients

serves 4

1 kg/2 lb 4 oz chicken wings,
  tips removed
2 celery sticks, chopped
700 ml/1¼ pints hot
  chicken stock
2 tbsp cornflour
3 tbsp white wine vinegar
  or rice vinegar
3 tbsp dark soy sauce
5 tbsp sweet chilli sauce
55 g/2 oz brown sugar
400 g/14 oz canned pineapple
  chunks in juice, drained
200 g/7 oz canned sliced bamboo
  shoots, drained and rinsed
½ yellow pepper, deseeded and
  thinly sliced
½ red pepper, deseeded and
  thinly sliced
salt

method

1 Preheat the slow cooker, if necessary, or according to the manufacturer's instructions.

2 Put the chicken wings and celery in the slow cooker and season with salt. Pour in the chicken stock, cover and cook on low for 5 hours.

3 Drain the chicken wings, reserving 350 ml/12 fl oz of the stock, and keep warm. Pour the reserved stock into a saucepan and stir in the cornflour. Add the vinegar, soy sauce and chilli sauce. Place over a medium heat and stir in the sugar. Cook, stirring constantly, for 5 minutes, or until the sugar has dissolved completely and the sauce is thickened, smooth and clear.

4 Lower the heat, stir in the pineapple, bamboo shoots and peppers and simmer gently for 2–3 minutes. Stir in the chicken wings until they are thoroughly coated, then transfer to serving bowls.

warm chickpea salad

ingredients

serves 4

225 g/8 oz dried chickpeas,
    soaked in water overnight, or
    for at least 5 hours
115 g/4 oz stoned black olives
4 spring onions, finely chopped
fresh parsley sprigs, to garnish
crusty bread, to serve

dressing

2 tbsp red wine vinegar
2 tbsp mixed chopped fresh herbs,
    such as parsley, rosemary
    and thyme
3 garlic cloves, very finely chopped
125 ml/4 fl oz extra virgin olive oil
salt and pepper

method

1 Preheat the slow cooker, if necessary, or according
  to the manufacturer's instructions.

2 Drain and rinse the beans, place in a saucepan, cover
  with fresh cold water, and bring to the boil. Boil rapidly
  for at least 10 minutes, then remove from the heat,
  drain and rinse again. Place the chickpeas in the slow
  cooker and add sufficient boiling water to cover. Cover
  and cook on low for 12 hours.

3 Drain well and transfer to a bowl. Stir in the olives
  and spring onions.

4 To make the dressing, whisk together the vinegar,
  herbs and garlic in a jug and season with salt and
  pepper to taste. Gradually whisk in the olive oil. Pour
  the dressing over the still-warm chickpeas and toss
  lightly to coat. Garnish with the parsley sprigs and
  serve warm with crusty bread.

boston baked beans

ingredients

serves 4–6

450 g/1 lb dried white haricot
  beans, soaked in water
  overnight, or for at least
  5 hours
115 g/4 oz salt pork, soaked in
  cold water for 3 hours
  and drained
3 tbsp black treacle
3 tbsp muscovado sugar
2 tsp dry mustard
1 onion, chopped
salt and pepper

method

1 Preheat the slow cooker, if necessary, or according to the manufacturer's instructions.

2 Drain and rinse the beans, place in a saucepan, cover with fresh cold water, and bring to the boil. Boil rapidly for at least 10 minutes, then remove from the heat, drain and rinse again. Place the beans in the slow cooker and add about 1.4 litres/2½ pints boiling water so that they are covered. Cover and cook the beans on high for 3 hours. Meanwhile, cut the salt pork into chunks.

3 Drain the beans, reserving 225 ml/8 fl oz of the cooking liquid. Mix the reserved liquid with the treacle, sugar, mustard and 1 teaspoon salt.

4 Return the beans to the slow cooker and add the salt pork, onion and the treacle mixture. Stir, then cover and cook on low for 11 hours. Adjust the seasoning and serve immediately.

louisiana courgettes

ingredients

serves 6

1 kg/2 lb 4 oz courgettes, thickly sliced
1 onion, finely chopped
2 garlic cloves, finely chopped
2 red peppers, deseeded and chopped
5 tbsp hot vegetable stock
4 tomatoes, peeled and chopped
25 g/1 oz butter, diced
salt and cayenne pepper

method

1 Preheat the slow cooker, if necessary, or according to the manufacturer's instructions.

2 Place the courgettes, onion, garlic and red peppers in the slow cooker and season to taste with salt and cayenne pepper. Pour in the stock and mix well.

3 Sprinkle the chopped tomatoes on top and dot with the butter. Cover and cook on high for 2½ hours until tender.

aubergine timbales

ingredients

serves 4

3 tbsp olive oil, plus extra
   for greasing
2 onions, finely chopped
2 aubergines, halved with flesh
   removed and shells reserved
2 red peppers, deseeded
   and chopped
1 large tomato, peeled
   and chopped
6 tbsp milk
2 egg yolks
pinch of ground cinnamon
85 g/3 oz crispbread, finely
   crushed
salt and pepper
sprigs of fresh coriander, to garnish

sauce

300 ml/10 fl oz soured cream
3–4 tbsp sun-dried tomato purée
   (optional)

method

1 Preheat the slow cooker, if necessary, or according
   to the manufacturer's instructions.

2 Heat the oil in a large, heavy-based frying pan. Add the
   onions and cook over a low heat for 5 minutes. Add
   the aubergine flesh, peppers and tomato and cook for
   15–20 minutes, until all the vegetables are soft. Transfer
   the mixture to a food processor or blender and process
   to a purée, then scrape into a bowl. Beat together the
   milk, egg yolks, cinnamon and salt and pepper in a jug,
   then stir into the vegetable purée.

3 Brush 4 ramekins or cups with oil and sprinkle with the
   crispbread crumbs to coat. Mix about three-quarters
   of the remaining crumbs into the vegetable purée.
   Slice the aubergine shells into strips and use them to
   line the ramekins. Spoon the filling into the ramekins,
   and fold the overlapping strips over the top.

4 Cover with foil and place in the slow cooker. Pour in
   boiling water to one-third of the way up the sides of
   the ramekins. Cover and cook on high for 2 hours.

5 To make the sauce, lightly beat the soured cream and
   add the tomato purée to taste, if using. Season with
   salt and pepper. Lift the ramekins out of the cooker
   and remove the foil. Invert onto serving plates and
   serve with the sauce, garnished with coriander sprigs.

cabbage roulades with tomato sauce

ingredients

serves 4

225 g/8 oz mixed nuts,
    finely ground
2 onions, finely chopped
2 garlic cloves, finely chopped
2 celery sticks, finely chopped
115 g/4 oz grated Cheddar cheese
1 tsp finely chopped thyme
2 eggs
1 tsp yeast extract
12 large green cabbage leaves

tomato sauce

2 tbsp sunflower oil
2 onions, chopped
2 garlic cloves, finely chopped
600 g/1 lb 5 oz canned
    chopped tomatoes
2 tbsp tomato purée
1½ tsp sugar
salt and pepper

method

1 Preheat the slow cooker, if necessary, or according to the manufacturer's instructions.

2 First make the tomato sauce. Heat the oil in a saucepan. Add the onions and cook over a medium heat, stirring occasionally, for 5 minutes until softened. Stir in the garlic and cook for 1 minute, then add the tomatoes, tomato purée and sugar. Season with salt and pepper and bring to the boil. Lower the heat and simmer gently for 20 minutes until thickened.

3 Meanwhile, mix together the nuts, onions, garlic, celery, cheese and thyme in a bowl. Lightly beat the eggs with the yeast extract in a jug, then stir into the nut mixture.

4 Cut out the thick stalks from the cabbage leaves. Blanch the leaves in a large saucepan of boiling water for 5 minutes, then drain and refresh under cold water. Pat dry with kitchen paper. Place a little of the nut mixture on the stalk end of each cabbage leaf. Fold the sides over, then roll up to make a neat parcel.

5 Arrange the parcels in the slow cooker, seam side down. Pour the sauce over the cabbage parcels. Cover and cook on low for 3–4 hours. Serve the cabbage roulades hot or cold.

everyday

parmesan chicken

ingredients

serves 4

1 egg, beaten
4 skinless, boneless chicken breasts
85 g/3 oz fine dry breadcrumbs
2 tbsp olive oil
350 g/12 oz ready-made
    tomato-based pasta sauce
4 thin slices Cheddar cheese
115 g/4 oz finely grated Parmesan
    cheese
salt and pepper
cooked rice, to serve

method

1 Preheat the slow cooker, if necessary, or according to the manufacturer's instructions.

2 Season the egg with salt and pepper. Dip each chicken breast in the egg, turning to coat evenly, then dip into the breadcrumbs, lightly pressing down to cover evenly.

3 Heat the oil in a frying pan over a high heat, add the chicken breasts and fry quickly for 3–4 minutes, until golden brown, turning once.

4 Pour the pasta sauce into the slow cooker and place the chicken breasts on top. Cover and cook on low for 4 hours.

5 Place a slice of Cheddar cheese on top of each chicken breast and sprinkle with Parmesan cheese. Cover and cook on high for a further 20 minutes. Serve immediately with rice.

chicken & dumplings

ingredients

serves 4

2 tbsp olive oil
1 large onion, thinly sliced
2 carrots, cut into 2-cm/³/₄-inch
    chunks
225 g/8 oz French beans,
    cut into 2.5-cm/1-inch lengths
4 skinless, boneless chicken breasts
300 ml/10 fl oz hot chicken stock
salt and pepper

dumplings

200 g/7 oz self-raising flour
100 g/3½ oz shredded suet
4 tbsp chopped fresh parsley

method.

1 Preheat the slow cooker, if necessary, or according to the manufacturer's instructions.

2 Heat 1 tablespoon of oil in a frying pan, add the onion and fry over a high heat for 3–4 minutes, or until golden. Place in the slow cooker with the carrots and beans.

3 Add the remaining oil to the pan, then add the chicken breasts and fry until golden, turning once. Arrange on top of the vegetables in a single layer, season well with salt and pepper and pour over the stock. Cover and cook on low for 4 hours.

4 Turn the slow cooker up to high while making the dumplings. Sift the flour into a bowl and stir in the suet and parsley. Season to taste with salt and pepper. Stir in just enough cold water to make a fairly firm dough, mixing lightly. Divide into 12 and shape into small balls.

5 Arrange the dumplings on top of the chicken, cover and cook for 30 minutes on high. Serve immediately.

chicken & sweetcorn stew

ingredients

serves 4

3 tbsp sunflower oil
1 large onion, thinly sliced
1 green pepper, deseeded
   and chopped
8 chicken pieces, such as thighs
   and drumsticks
400 g/14 oz canned chopped
   tomatoes, drained
pinch of cayenne pepper
1 tbsp Worcestershire sauce
300 ml/10 fl oz hot chicken stock
1 tbsp cornflour
200 g/7 oz frozen sweetcorn,
   thawed
450 g/1 lb frozen broad beans,
   thawed
salt
crusty bread, to serve

method

1 Preheat the slow cooker, if necessary, or according to the manufacturer's instructions.

2 Heat the oil in a large, heavy-based frying pan. Add the onion and green pepper and cook over a medium heat, stirring occasionally, for 5 minutes until the onion is softened. Using a slotted spoon, transfer the mixture to the slow cooker.

3 Add the chicken to the pan and cook, turning occasionally, for 5 minutes until golden all over. Transfer to the slow cooker and add the tomatoes. Season with cayenne pepper and salt. Stir the Worcestershire sauce into the hot stock and pour into the slow cooker. Cover and cook on low for 6½ hours.

4 Mix the cornflour to a paste with 2–3 tablespoons water and stir into the stew. Add the sweetcorn and beans, re-cover and cook on high for 30–40 minutes until everything is cooked through and piping hot. Transfer the stew to warmed bowls and serve with crusty bread.

chicken braised with red cabbage

ingredients

serves 4

2 tbsp sunflower oil
4 skinless chicken thighs
    or drumsticks
1 onion, chopped
500 g/1 lb 2 oz red cabbage,
    cored and shredded
2 apples, peeled and chopped
12 canned or cooked chestnuts,
    halved (optional)
½ tsp juniper berries
125 ml/4 fl oz red wine
salt and pepper
fresh flat-leaf parsley, to garnish

method

1 Preheat the slow cooker, if necessary, or according to the manufacturer's instructions.

2 Heat the oil in a large, heavy-based saucepan. Add the chicken and cook, turning frequently, for 5 minutes until golden on all sides. Using a slotted spoon, transfer to a plate lined with kitchen paper.

3 Add the onion to the saucepan and cook over a medium heat, stirring occasionally, until softened. Stir in the cabbage and apples and cook, stirring occasionally, for 5 minutes. Add the chestnuts, if using, juniper berries and wine and season to taste with salt and pepper. Bring to the boil.

4 Spoon half the cabbage mixture into the slow cooker, add the chicken pieces, then top with the remaining cabbage mixture. Cover and cook on low for 5 hours until the chicken is tender and cooked through. Serve immediately, garnished with the parsley.

chicken & apple pot

ingredients

serves 4

1 tbsp olive oil
4 chicken portions, about
    175 g/6 oz each
1 onion, chopped
2 celery sticks, coarsely chopped
1½ tbsp plain flour
300 ml/10 fl oz clear apple juice
150 ml/5 fl oz chicken stock
1 cooking apple, cored and
    cut into quarters
2 bay leaves
1–2 tsp clear honey
1 yellow pepper, deseeded
    and cut into chunks
salt and pepper

garnish

1 large or 2 medium eating apples,
    cored and sliced
1 tbsp butter, melted
2 tbsp demerara sugar
1 tbsp chopped fresh mint

method

1 Preheat the slow cooker, if necessary, or according to the manufacturer's instructions.

2 Heat the oil in a heavy-based frying pan. Add the chicken and cook over a medium–high heat, for 10 minutes, until golden brown all over. Using a slotted spoon, transfer the chicken to the slow cooker.

3 Add the onion and celery to the pan and cook over a low heat, stirring occasionally, for 5 minutes, until softened. Sprinkle in the flour and cook, stirring constantly, for 2 minutes, then remove the pan from the heat. Stir in the apple juice and stock, then return the pan to the heat and bring to the boil, stirring constantly. Stir in the apple, bay leaves and honey and season to taste with salt and pepper.

4 Pour the mixture over the chicken, cover the slow cooker and cook on low for 6½ hours, until the chicken is tender and the juices run clear when the thickest part is pierced with a sharp knife. Stir in the yellow pepper, re-cover and cook on high for 45 minutes.

5 Preheat the grill. Brush the apple slices with the melted butter and sprinkle them with sugar. Grill for 2 minutes on each side until the sugar has caramelized. Serve the stew garnished with the caramelized apple slices and the mint.

turkey hash

ingredients

serves 4

1 tbsp olive oil
500 g/1 lb 2 oz turkey mince
1 large red onion, diced
550 g/1 lb 4 oz butternut
   squash, diced
2 celery sticks, sliced
500 g/1 lb 2 oz potatoes,
   peeled and diced
3 tbsp Worcestershire sauce
2 bay leaves
salt and pepper

method

1 Preheat the slow cooker, if necessary, or according to the manufacturer's instructions.

2 Heat the oil in a frying pan, add the turkey and fry over a high heat, stirring, until broken up and lightly browned all over.

3 Place all the vegetables in the slow cooker then add the turkey and pan juices. Add the Worcestershire sauce and bay leaves and season with salt and pepper. Cover and cook on low for 7 hours. Serve immediately.

turkey & rice casserole

ingredients

serves 4

1 tbsp olive oil
500 g/1 lb 2 oz diced
    turkey breast
1 onion, diced
2 carrots, diced
2 celery sticks, sliced
250 g/9 oz closed-cup
    mushrooms, sliced
175 g/6 oz long-grain rice,
    preferably Basmati
450 ml/16 fl oz hot chicken stock
salt and pepper

method

1　Preheat the slow cooker, if necessary, or according to the manufacturer's instructions.

2　Heat the oil in a heavy-based frying pan, add the turkey and fry over a high heat for 3–4 minutes, until lightly browned.

3　Combine the onion, carrots, celery, mushrooms and rice in the slow cooker. Arrange the turkey on top, season well with salt and pepper and pour the stock over. Cover and cook on high for 2 hours.

4　Stir lightly with a fork to mix, adjust the seasoning to taste and serve immediately.

pesto turkey pasta bake

ingredients

serves 4

250 g/9 oz dried macaroni
175 ml/6 fl oz tomato juice
500 g/1 lb 2 oz turkey mince
1 small onion, finely chopped
40 g/1½ oz fresh white
    breadcrumbs
100 g/3½ oz pesto sauce
125 g/4½ oz mozzarella cheese
salt and pepper
fresh basil leaves, to garnish

method

1 Preheat the slow cooker, if necessary, or according to the manufacturer's instructions.

2 Bring a large saucepan of lightly salted water to the boil, add the pasta, return to the boil and cook for half the amount of time stated on the pack (5–6 minutes). Drain well, place in the slow cooker and stir in the tomato juice.

3 Mix the turkey, onion and breadcrumbs together. Season well with salt and pepper. Divide the mixture into about 20 small balls, rolling them with your hands.

4 Arrange the meatballs over the pasta in a single layer and spoon a little of the pesto sauce on top of each. Cover and cook on high for 2 hours.

5 Tear the mozzarella cheese into small pieces and scatter over the meatballs. Cover and cook on high for a further 20 minutes. Serve immediately, garnished with fresh basil.

pot roast with beer

ingredients

serves 4-6

2 small onions, each cut
    into 8 wedges
8 small carrots, halved
    lengthways
1 fennel bulb, cut into 8 wedges
2.25 kg/5 lb rolled chuck steak
2 tbsp Dijon mustard
1 tbsp plain flour
100 ml/3½ fl oz beer
salt and pepper

method

1 Preheat the slow cooker, if necessary, or according to the manufacturer's instructions.

2 Place the onions, carrots and fennel in the slow cooker and season to taste with salt and pepper. Place the beef on top.

3 Mix the mustard and flour together to form a paste and spread over the beef. Season well and pour over the beer. Cover and cook on low for 8 hours.

4 Carefully remove the beef and vegetables and place on a warmed platter. Skim the excess fat from the juices and pour into a jug to serve with the beef.

spicy beef

ingredients

serves 4

1½ tbsp plain flour
450 g/1 lb stewing steak,
    cut into 2.5-cm/1-inch cubes
2 tbsp olive oil
1 Spanish onion, chopped
3–4 garlic cloves, crushed
1 green chilli, deseeded
    and chopped
3 celery sticks, sliced
4 cloves
1 tsp ground allspice
1–2 tsp hot pepper sauce
600 ml/1 pint beef stock
225 g/8 oz peeled acorn or other
    squash, cut into small chunks
1 large red pepper, deseeded
    and chopped
4 tomatoes, coarsely chopped
115 g/4 oz okra, trimmed
    and halved
mixed wild and long-grain rice,
    to serve

method

1 Preheat the slow cooker, if necessary, or according to the manufacturer's instructions.

2 Spread out the flour in a shallow dish, add the steak cubes and toss until well coated. Shake off any excess and reserve the remaining flour.

3 Heat the oil in a heavy-based frying pan. Add the onion, garlic, chilli, celery, cloves and allspice and cook over a low heat, stirring occasionally, for 5 minutes until the vegetables have softened. Increase the heat to high, add the steak cubes and cook, stirring frequently, for 3 minutes until browned all over. Sprinkle in the reserved flour and cook, stirring constantly, for 2 minutes, then remove the pan from the heat.

4 Stir in the hot pepper sauce, then gradually stir in the stock. Return the pan to the heat and bring to the boil, stirring constantly. Transfer the mixture to the slow cooker and add the squash. Cover and cook on low for 8 hours.

5 Add the red pepper, tomatoes and okra, re-cover and cook on high for 1 hour. Serve with mixed wild and long-grain rice.

beef & button onions

ingredients

serves 4-6

2 tbsp olive oil
450 g/1 lb button onions,
    peeled but left whole
2 garlic cloves, halved
900 g/2 lb stewing beef, cubed
½ tsp ground cinnamon
1 tsp ground cloves
1 tsp ground cumin
2 tbsp tomato purée
75 cl bottle red wine
grated rind and juice of 1 orange
1 bay leaf
salt and pepper
1 tbsp chopped fresh flat-leaf
    parsley, to garnish
boiled new potatoes, to serve

method

1 Preheat the slow cooker, if necessary, or according to the manufacturer's instructions.

2 Heat the oil in a heavy-based frying pan. Add the onions and garlic and cook over a medium heat, stirring frequently, for 5 minutes until softened and beginning to brown. Increase the heat to high, add the beef and cook, stirring frequently, for 5 minutes, until browned all over.

3 Stir in the cinnamon, cloves, cumin and tomato purée and season with salt and pepper. Pour in the wine, scraping up any sediment from the base of the frying pan. Stir in the orange rind and juice, add the bay leaf and bring to the boil.

4 Transfer the mixture to the slow cooker, cover and cook on low for 9 hours, until the beef is tender. If possible, stir the stew once during the second half of the cooking time.

5 Serve the stew garnished with the parsley and accompanied by boiled new potatoes.

provençal beef & olives

ingredients

serves 4–6

900 g/2 lb stewing steak, cubed
2 onions, thinly sliced
2 carrots, sliced
4 large garlic cloves, lightly
    crushed
1 bouquet garni
4 juniper berries
500 ml/18 fl oz dry red wine
2 tbsp brandy
2 tbsp olive oil
3 tbsp plain flour
175 g/6 oz lardons or diced bacon
2 x 10-cm/4-inch strips of thinly
    pared orange rind
85 g/3 oz stoned black olives,
    rinsed
salt and pepper
1 tbsp chopped fresh flat-leaf
    parsley and 1 tbsp finely grated
    orange rind, to garnish
tagliatelle or buttered noodles,
    to serve

method

1 Preheat the slow cooker, if necessary, or according to the manufacturer's instructions.

2 Put the stewing steak in a large, non-metallic dish. Add the onions, carrots, garlic, bouquet garni and juniper berries and season with salt and pepper. Combine the wine, brandy and olive oil in a jug and pour the mixture over the meat and vegetables. Cover with clingfilm and marinate in the refrigerator for 24 hours.

3 Using a slotted spoon, remove the steak from the marinade and pat dry with kitchen paper. Reserve the marinade, vegetables and flavourings. Place the flour in a shallow dish and season well with salt and pepper. Toss the steak cubes in the flour until well coated and shake off any excess.

4 Sprinkle half the lardons in the base of the slow cooker and top with the steak cubes. Pour in the marinade, including the vegetables and flavourings, and add the strips of orange rind and the olives. Top with the remaining lardons. Cover and cook on low for 9½–10 hours, until the steak and vegetables are tender.

5 Remove and discard the bouquet garni and skim off any fat that has risen to the surface of the stew. Sprinkle the parsley and grated orange rind over the top and serve with tagliatelle or buttered noodles.

goulash

ingredients

serves 4

4 tbsp sunflower oil
650 g/1 lb 7 oz braising steak,
    cut into 2.5-cm/1-inch cubes
2 tsp plain flour
2 tsp paprika
300 ml/10 fl oz beef stock
3 onions, chopped
4 carrots, diced
1 large potato or 2 medium
    potatoes, diced
1 bay leaf
½–1 tsp caraway seeds
400 g/14 oz canned
    chopped tomatoes
2 tbsp soured cream
salt and pepper

method

1 Preheat the slow cooker, if necessary, or according to the manufacturer's instructions.

2 Heat half the oil in a heavy-based frying pan. Add the beef and cook over a medium heat, stirring frequently, until browned all over. Lower the heat and stir in the flour and paprika. Cook, stirring constantly, for 2 minutes. Gradually stir in the stock and bring to the boil, then transfer the mixture to the slow cooker.

3 Rinse out the frying pan and heat the remaining oil in it. Add the onions and cook over a low heat, stirring occasionally, for 5 minutes until softened. Stir in the carrots and potato and cook for a few minutes more. Add the bay leaf, caraway seeds and tomatoes with their can juices. Season with salt and pepper.

4 Transfer the vegetable mixture to the slow cooker, stir well, then cover and cook on low for 9 hours until the meat is tender.

5 Remove and discard the bay leaf. Pour over the soured cream and serve immediately.

variation

For a slightly sweeter spice, substitute 1 teaspoon of paprika for sweet paprika and add 1 teaspoon of sugar.

lamb with red peppers

ingredients

serves 4

1½ tbsp plain flour
1 tsp ground cloves
450 g/1 lb boneless lamb, cut into thin strips
1–1½ tbsp olive oil
1 white onion, sliced
2–3 garlic cloves, sliced
300 ml/10 fl oz orange juice
150 ml/5 fl oz lamb or chicken stock
1 cinnamon stick
2 red peppers, deseeded and sliced into rings
4 tomatoes
4 fresh coriander sprigs
salt and pepper
1 tbsp chopped fresh coriander, to garnish
mashed sweet potatoes mixed with chopped spring onions and green beans, to serve

method

1 Preheat the slow cooker, if necessary, or according to the manufacturer's instructions.

2 Combine the flour and ground cloves in a shallow dish, add the strips of lamb and toss well to coat, shaking off any excess. Reserve the remaining spiced flour.

3 Heat 1 tablespoon of the oil in a heavy-based frying pan, add the lamb and cook over a high heat, stirring frequently, for 3 minutes, until browned all over. Using a slotted spoon, transfer the lamb to the slow cooker. Add the onion and garlic to the frying pan, with the remaining oil if necessary, and cook over a low heat, stirring occasionally, for 5 minutes, until softened. Sprinkle in the reserved spiced flour and cook, stirring constantly, for 2 minutes, then remove the pan from the heat. Stir in the orange juice and stock, then return the pan to the heat and bring to the boil, stirring constantly.

4 Pour the mixture over the lamb, add the cinnamon stick, red peppers, tomatoes and coriander sprigs and stir well. Cover and cook on low for 7–8 hours until the meat is tender. Remove and discard the cinnamon stick and coriander sprigs. Season to taste with salt and pepper, sprinkle the stew with chopped coriander and serve with mashed sweet potatoes with spring onions and green beans.

ham with black-eyed beans

ingredients

serves 4

2–3 tbsp olive oil
550 g/1 lb 4 oz lean gammon, trimmed and cut into 4-cm/1½-inch pieces
1 onion, chopped
2–3 garlic cloves, chopped
2 celery sticks, chopped
175 g/6 oz carrots, thinly sliced
1 cinnamon stick
½ tsp ground cloves
¼ tsp freshly grated nutmeg
1 tsp dried oregano
450 ml/16 fl oz chicken or vegetable stock
2 tbsp maple syrup
225 g/8 oz chorizo or other spicy sausages, skinned
400 g/14 oz canned black-eyed beans, drained and rinsed
1 orange pepper, deseeded and chopped
1 tbsp cornflour
pepper
sprig of fresh flat-leaf parsley or oregano, to garnish

method

1 Preheat the slow cooker, if necessary, or according to the manufacturer's instructions.

2 Heat 1 tablespoon of the oil in a heavy-based frying pan, add the gammon and cook over a high heat, stirring frequently, for 5 minutes until browned all over. Using a slotted spoon, transfer to the slow cooker.

3 Add 1 tablespoon of the remaining oil to the frying pan. Reduce the heat to low, add the onion, garlic, celery and carrots and cook, stirring occasionally, for 5 minutes until softened. Add the cinnamon, cloves and nutmeg, season with pepper and cook, stirring constantly, for 2 minutes. Stir in the dried oregano, stock and maple syrup and bring to the boil, stirring constantly. Pour the mixture over the gammon, stir well, cover and cook on low for 5–6 hours.

4 Heat the remaining oil in a frying pan, add the chorizo and cook for 10 minutes, until browned all over. Remove from the pan, cut each into 3–4 chunks and add to the slow cooker with the black-eyed beans and orange pepper. Re-cover and cook on high for 1–1½ hours. Stir the cornflour with 2 tablespoons water to a smooth paste in a bowl, then stir into the stew, re-cover and cook on high for 15 minutes. Discard the cinnamon stick, garnish the stew with a fresh herb sprig and serve.

tagliatelle with prawns

ingredients

serves 4

400 g/14 oz tomatoes,
    peeled and chopped
140 g/5 oz tomato purée
1 garlic clove, finely chopped
2 tbsp chopped fresh parsley
500 g/1 lb 2 oz cooked, peeled
    Mediterranean prawns
6 fresh basil leaves, torn
400 g/14 oz dried tagliatelle
salt and pepper
fresh basil leaves, to garnish

method

1 Preheat the slow cooker, if necessary, or according to the manufacturer's instructions.

2 Put the tomatoes, tomato purée, garlic and parsley in the slow cooker and season with salt and pepper. Cover and cook on low for 7 hours.

3 Add the prawns and basil. Re-cover and cook on high for 15 minutes.

4 Meanwhile, bring a large saucepan of lightly salted water to the boil. Add the pasta, bring back to the boil and cook for 10–12 minutes until tender but still firm to the bite.

5 Drain the pasta and tip it into a warmed serving bowl. Add the prawn sauce and toss lightly with 2 large forks. Garnish with the basil leaves and serve immediately.

spiced seafood & okra

ingredients

serves 6

2 tbsp sunflower oil

175 g/6 oz okra, trimmed and
    cut into 2.5-cm/1-inch pieces

2 onions, finely chopped

4 celery sticks, very finely chopped

1 garlic clove, finely chopped

2 tbsp plain flour

½ tsp sugar

1 tsp ground cumin

700 ml/1¼ pints fish stock

1 red pepper, deseeded and
    chopped

1 green pepper, deseeded
    and chopped

2 large tomatoes, chopped

4 tbsp chopped fresh parsley

1 tbsp chopped fresh coriander

dash of Tabasco

350 g/12 oz large raw prawns,
    peeled and deveined

350 g/12 oz cod or haddock fillets,
    skinned and cut into 2.5-cm/
    1-inch chunks

350 g/12 oz monkfish fillet,
    cut into 2.5-cm/1-inch chunks

salt and pepper

method

1 Preheat the slow cooker, if necessary, or according
to the manufacturer's instructions.

2 Heat half the oil in a heavy-based frying pan. Add the
okra and cook over a low heat, stirring frequently, for
5 minutes until browned. Using a slotted spoon,
transfer the okra to the slow cooker.

3 Add the remaining oil to the frying pan. Add the
onions and celery and cook over a low heat, stirring
occasionally, for 5 minutes until softened. Add the
garlic and cook, stirring frequently, for 1 minute, then
sprinkle in the flour, sugar and cumin and season with
salt and pepper. Cook, stirring constantly, for 2 minutes,
then remove the frying pan from the heat.

4 Gradually stir in the stock, then return the pan to the
heat and bring to the boil, stirring constantly. Pour
the mixture over the okra and stir in the peppers and
tomatoes. Cover and cook on low for 5–6 hours.

5 Stir in the parsley, coriander and Tabasco to taste, then
add the prawns, cod and monkfish. Cover and cook
on high for 30 minutes until the fish and prawns are
ready. Taste and adjust the seasoning if necessary
and serve.

south-western seafood

ingredients

serves 4

2 tbsp olive oil, plus extra
    for drizzling
1 large onion, chopped
4 garlic cloves, finely chopped
1 yellow pepper, deseeded
    and chopped
1 red pepper, deseeded
    and chopped
1 orange pepper, deseeded
    and chopped
450 g/1 lb tomatoes,
    peeled and chopped
2 large, mild green chillies,
    such as poblano, chopped
finely grated rind and
    juice of 1 lime
2 tbsp chopped fresh coriander,
    plus extra leaves to garnish
1 bay leaf
450 ml/16 fl oz fish, vegetable
    or chicken stock
450 g/1 lb red mullet fillets
450 g/1 lb raw prawns
225 g/8 oz prepared squid
salt and pepper

method

1 Preheat the slow cooker, if necessary, or according
to the manufacturer's instructions.

2 Heat the oil in a saucepan. Add the onion and garlic
and cook over a low heat, stirring occasionally, for
5 minutes until softened. Add the peppers, tomatoes
and chillies and cook, stirring frequently, for 5 minutes.
Stir in the lime rind and juice, add the coriander and
bay leaf and pour in the stock. Bring the mixture to
a boil, stirring occasionally.

3 Transfer the mixture to the slow cooker, cover and
cook on low for $7\frac{1}{2}$ hours. Meanwhile, skin the fish
fillets, if necessary, and cut the flesh into chunks. Shell
and devein the prawns. Cut the squid bodies into rings
and halve the tentacles or leave them whole.

4 Add the seafood to the stew, season with salt and
pepper, re-cover and cook on high for 30 minutes,
or until the seafood is tender and cooked through.
Remove and discard the bay leaf, garnish the stew
with coriander leaves and serve.

tagliatelle with tuna

ingredients

serves 4

200 g/7 oz dried egg tagliatelle
400 g/14 oz canned tuna
    steak in oil, drained
1 bunch spring onions, sliced
175 g/6 oz frozen peas
2 tsp hot chilli sauce
600 ml/1 pint hot chicken stock
115 g/4 oz grated Cheddar cheese
salt and pepper

method

1 Preheat the slow cooker, if necessary, or according to the manufacturer's instructions.

2 Bring a large saucepan of lightly salted water to the boil. Add the pasta, return to the boil and cook for 2 minutes, until the pasta ribbons are loose. Drain.

3 Break up the tuna into bite-sized chunks and place in the slow cooker with the pasta, spring onions and peas. Season to taste with salt and pepper.

4 Add the chilli sauce to the stock and pour over the ingredients in the slow cooker. Sprinkle the grated cheese over the top. Cover and cook on low for 2 hours. Serve immediately on warmed plates.

spring vegetables

ingredients

serves 4

2 tbsp olive oil

4–8 baby onions, halved

2 celery sticks, cut into 5-mm/¼-inch slices

225 g/8 oz young carrots, halved if large

300 g/10½ oz new potatoes, halved

850 ml–1.2 litres/1½–2 pints vegetable stock

225 g/8 oz dried haricot beans, soaked in water overnight, or for at least 5 hours

1 bouquet garni

1½–2 tbsp light soy sauce

85 g/3 oz baby sweetcorn

115 g/4 oz shelled broad beans, thawed if frozen

225 g/8 oz Savoy cabbage, shredded

1½ tbsp cornflour

salt and pepper

55–85 g/2–3 oz freshly grated Parmesan cheese, to serve

method

1 Preheat the slow cooker, if necessary, or according to the manufacturer's instructions.

2 Drain and rinse the beans, place in a saucepan, cover with fresh cold water, and bring to the boil. Boil rapidly for at least 10 minutes, then remove from the heat, drain and rinse again.

3 Heat the oil in a saucepan. Add the onions, celery, carrots and potatoes and cook over a low heat, stirring frequently, for 5–8 minutes until softened. Add the stock, haricot beans, bouquet garni and soy sauce, bring to the boil, then transfer to the slow cooker.

4 Add the corn, broad beans and cabbage, season with salt and pepper and stir well. Cover and cook on high for 3–4 hours until the vegetables are tender.

5 Remove and discard the bouquet garni. Stir the cornflour with 3 tablespoons water to a paste in a small bowl, then stir into the stew. Re-cover and cook on high for a further 15 minutes until thickened. Serve the stew with the Parmesan handed separately.

vegetable hotpot with parsley dumplings

ingredients

serves 6

½ swede, cut into chunks
2 onions, sliced
2 potatoes, cut into chunks
2 carrots, cut into chunks
2 celery sticks, sliced
2 courgettes, sliced
2 tbsp tomato purée
600 ml/1 pint hot vegetable stock
1 bay leaf
1 tsp ground coriander
½ tsp dried thyme
salt and pepper
fresh coriander sprigs, to garnish

parsley dumplings
200 g/7 oz self-raising flour
115 g/4 oz vegetable suet
2 tbsp chopped fresh parsley
125 ml/4 fl oz milk

method

1 Preheat the slow cooker, if necessary, or according to the manufacturer's instructions.

2 Put the swede, onions, potatoes, carrots, celery and courgettes into the slow cooker. Stir the tomato purée into the stock and pour it over the vegetables. Add the bay leaf, ground coriander and thyme and season with salt and pepper. Cover and cook on low for 6 hours.

3 To make the dumplings, sift the flour with a pinch of salt into a bowl and stir in the suet and parsley. Add just enough milk to make a firm but light dough. Knead lightly and shape into 12 small balls.

4 Place the dumplings on top of the stew. Cook on high for 30 minutes. Remove and discard the bay leaf and garnish with coriander sprigs. Serve immediately.

winter vegetables

ingredients

serves 4

2 tbsp sunflower oil
2 onions, chopped
3 carrots, halved lengthways
3 parsnips, halved lengthways
2 bunches celery, cut into long
   chunks
2 tbsp chopped fresh parsley
1 tbsp chopped fresh coriander
300 ml/10 fl oz vegetable stock
salt and pepper

method

1 Preheat the slow cooker, if necessary, or according to the manufacturer's instructions.

2 Heat the oil in a large, heavy-based saucepan. Add the onions and cook over a medium heat, stirring occasionally, for 5 minutes until softened. Add the carrots, parsnips and celery and cook, stirring occasionally, for a further 5 minutes. Stir in the herbs, season with salt and pepper and pour in the stock. Bring to the boil.

3 Transfer the vegetable mixture to the slow cooker, cover and cook on high for 3 hours until tender. Taste and adjust the seasoning if necessary. Using a slotted spoon, transfer the vegetables to warmed plates, then spoon over a little of the cooking liquid. Garnish with a few of the reserved celery leaves.

vegetables & lentils

ingredients

serves 4

1 onion
10 cloves
225 g/8 oz Puy or green lentils
1 bay leaf
1.5 litres/2¾ pints vegetable
    stock
2 leeks, sliced
2 potatoes, diced
2 carrots, chopped
3 courgettes, sliced
1 celery stick, sliced
1 red pepper, deseeded
    and chopped
1 tbsp lemon juice
salt and pepper

method

1 Preheat the slow cooker, if necessary, or according to the manufacturer's instructions.

2 Peel the onion, stud it with the cloves and place it in the slow cooker. Add the lentils and bay leaf, pour in the stock, cover and cook on high for 1½–2 hours.

3 Remove the onion with a slotted spoon and re-cover the slow cooker. Remove and discard the cloves and slice the onion. Add the onion, leeks, potatoes, carrots, courgettes, celery and red pepper to the lentils. Season with salt and pepper, re-cover and cook on high for 3–4 hours until all the vegetables are tender.

4 Remove and discard the bay leaf and stir in the lemon juice. Taste and adjust the seasoning if necessary, then serve.

baked aubergine with courgette & tomato

ingredients

serves 4

2 large aubergines
olive oil, for brushing
2 large courgettes, sliced
4 tomatoes, sliced
1 garlic clove, finely chopped
15 g/½ oz dry breadcrumbs
15 g/½ oz grated Parmesan cheese
salt and pepper
freshly torn basil leaves,
     to garnish

method

1 Preheat the slow cooker, if necessary, or according to the manufacturer's instructions.

2 Cut the aubergines into fairly thin slices and brush with oil. Heat a large griddle pan or heavy-based frying pan over a high heat, then add the aubergines and cook in batches for 6–8 minutes, turning once, until soft and brown.

3 Layer the aubergines in the slow cooker with the courgettes, tomatoes and garlic, seasoning with salt and pepper between the layers.

4 Mix the breadcrumbs with the cheese and sprinkle over the vegetables. Cover and cook on low for 4 hours. Serve hot, garnished with basil.

four bean chilli

ingredients

serves 4-6

2 tbsp olive oil
1 onion, chopped
2–4 garlic cloves, chopped
2 red chillies, deseeded
  and chopped
225 g/8 oz drained canned red
  kidney beans, rinsed
225 g/8 oz drained canned
  chickpeas, rinsed
225 g/8 oz drained canned
  haricot beans, rinsed
1 tbsp tomato purée
700 ml/1¼ pints vegetable stock
1 red pepper, deseeded
  and chopped
4 tomatoes, coarsely chopped
175 g/6 oz shelled broad beans,
  thawed if frozen
1 tbsp chopped fresh coriander
soured cream, to serve
sprigs of fresh coriander and pinch
  of paprika, to garnish

method

1 Preheat the slow cooker, if necessary, or according
  to the manufacturer's instructions.

2 Heat the oil in a heavy-based frying pan. Add the
  onion, garlic and chillies and cook over a low heat,
  stirring occasionally, for 5 minutes until softened. Add
  the kidney beans, chickpeas and haricot beans. Mix
  together the tomato purée with a little of the stock in
  a jug and pour it over the beans. Add the remaining
  stock and bring to the boil.

3 Transfer the mixture to the slow cooker, cover and
  cook on low for 3 hours. Stir in the red pepper,
  tomatoes, broad beans and chopped coriander,
  re-cover and cook on high for 1–1½ hours until all
  the beans are tender.

4 Serve the stew topped with spoonfuls of soured cream
  and garnished with coriander sprigs and a sprinkling
  of paprika.

entertaining

chunky beef chilli

ingredients

serves 4

250 g/9 oz dried red kidney beans,
    soaked in water overnight, or
    for at least 5 hours
600 ml/1 pint cold water
2 garlic cloves, chopped
5 tbsp tomato purée
1 small green chilli, chopped
2 tsp ground cumin
2 tsp ground coriander
600 g/1 lb 5 oz chuck steak, diced
1 large onion, chopped
1 large green pepper, deseeded
    and sliced
salt and pepper
soured cream, to serve

method

1 Preheat the slow cooker, if necessary, or according
to the manufacturer's instructions.

2 Drain the beans and place in a saucepan, cover with
cold water and bring to the boil. Boil rapidly for
10 minutes, then remove from the heat and drain.
Place the beans in the slow cooker and add the cold
water to cover.

3 Mix the garlic, tomato purée, chilli, cumin and
coriander together in a large bowl. Add the steak,
onion and green pepper and mix to coat evenly.

4 Place the meat and vegetables on top of the beans,
cover and cook on low for 9 hours, until the beans and
meat are tender.

5 Stir, season to taste with salt and pepper and serve
with soured cream.

traditional pot roast

ingredients

serves 4–6

1 onion, finely chopped
4 carrots, sliced
4 baby turnips, sliced
4 celery sticks, sliced
2 potatoes, peeled and sliced
1 sweet potato, peeled and sliced
1.3–1.8 kg/3–4 lb topside of beef
1 bouquet garni
300 ml/10 fl oz hot beef stock
salt and pepper
sprig of fresh thyme, to garnish

method.

1 Preheat the slow cooker, if necessary, or according to the manufacturer's instructions.

2 Place the onion, carrots, turnips, celery, potatoes and sweet potato in the slow cooker and stir to mix well.

3 Rub the beef all over with salt and pepper, then place on top of the bed of vegetables. Add the bouquet garni and pour in the stock. Cover and cook on low for 9–10 hours until the beef is cooked to your liking.

4 Remove the beef, carve into slices and arrange on serving plates. Remove and discard the bouquet garni. Spoon some of the vegetables and cooking juices onto the plates and serve.

duckling with apples

ingredients

serves 6

1.8–2 kg/4–4 lb 8 oz duckling,
    cut into 8 pieces
2 tbsp olive oil
1 onion, finely chopped
1 carrot, finely chopped
300 ml/10 fl oz chicken stock
300 ml/10 fl oz dry white wine
bouquet garni
4 eating apples
55 g/2 oz unsalted butter
salt and pepper

method

1 Preheat the slow cooker, if necessary, or according to the manufacturer's instructions.

2 Season the duckling pieces with salt and pepper. Heat the oil in a large, heavy-based frying pan. Add all the duckling pieces, placing the breast portions skin side down. Cook over a medium–high heat for a few minutes until golden brown, then transfer the breast portions to a plate. Turn the other pieces and continue to cook until browned all over. Transfer to the plate.

3 Add the onion and carrot to the frying pan and cook over a low heat, stirring occasionally, for 5 minutes until the onion is softened. Add the stock and wine and bring to the boil.

4 Transfer the vegetable mixture to the slow cooker. Add the duckling pieces and the bouquet garni. Cover and cook on low for 8 hours, occasionally skimming off the fat from the slow cooker and replacing the lid each time. Shortly before you are ready to serve, peel, core and slice the apples. Melt the butter in a large frying pan. Add the apple slices and cook over a medium heat, turning occasionally, for 5 minutes until golden.

5 Spoon the cooked apples onto warmed plates and divide the duckling among them. Strain the sauce into a jug, then pour it over the duckling and serve.

lamb tagine

ingredients

serves 6

3 tbsp olive oil
2 red onions, chopped
2 garlic cloves, finely chopped
2.5-cm/1-inch piece fresh
    ginger, finely chopped
1 yellow pepper, deseeded
    and chopped
1 kg/2 lb 4 oz boneless shoulder
    of lamb, trimmed and cut
    into 2.5-cm/1-inch cubes
850 ml/1½ pints lamb or
    chicken stock
225 g/8 oz ready-to-eat
    dried apricots, halved
1 tbsp clear honey
4 tbsp lemon juice
pinch of saffron threads
5-cm/2-inch cinnamon stick
salt and pepper
55 g/2 oz flaked almonds, toasted
sprigs of fresh coriander, to garnish

method

1 Preheat the slow cooker, if necessary, or according to the manufacturer's instructions.

2 Heat the oil in a large, heavy-based saucepan. Add the onions, garlic, ginger and yellow pepper and cook over a low heat, stirring occasionally, for 5 minutes until the onion has softened. Add the lamb and stir well to mix, then pour in the stock. Add the apricots, honey, lemon juice, saffron and cinnamon stick and season with the salt and pepper. Bring to the boil.

3 Transfer the mixture to the slow cooker. Cover and cook on low for 8½ hours until the meat is tender.

4 Remove and discard the cinnamon stick. Transfer to warmed serving bowls, sprinkle with the almonds, garnish with fresh coriander and serve.

springtime lamb with asparagus

ingredients

serves 6

2 tbsp sunflower oil
1 onion, thinly sliced
2 garlic cloves, very finely chopped
1 kg/2 lb 4 oz boneless
    shoulder of lamb, cut into
    2.5-cm/1-in cubes
225 g/8 oz asparagus spears,
    thawed if frozen
300 ml/10 fl oz chicken stock
4 tbsp lemon juice
150 ml/5 fl oz double cream
salt and pepper

method

1 Preheat the slow cooker, if necessary, or according
   to the manufacturer's instructions.

2 Heat the oil in a large, heavy-based frying pan. Add
   the onion and cook over a medium heat, stirring
   occasionally, for 5 minutes until softened. Add the
   garlic and lamb and cook, stirring occasionally, for
   a further 5 minutes until the lamb is lightly browned
   all over.

3 Meanwhile, trim off and reserve the tips of the
   asparagus spears. Cut the stalks into 2–3 pieces.
   Add the stock and lemon juice to the frying pan,
   season with salt and pepper and bring to the boil.
   Lower the heat, add the asparagus stalks and simmer
   for 2 minutes.

4 Transfer the mixture to the slow cooker. Cover and
   cook on low for 7 hours until the lamb is tender.

5 About 20 minutes before you intend to serve, cook the
   reserved asparagus tips in a saucepan of lightly salted
   boiling water for 5 minutes. Drain well, then mix with
   the cream. Spoon the cream mixture on top of the
   lamb mixture but do not stir it in. Re-cover and cook on
   high for 15–20 minutes to heat through before serving.

lamb shanks with olives

ingredients

serves 4

1½ tbsp plain flour
4 lamb shanks
2 tbsp olive oil
1 onion, sliced
2 garlic cloves, finely chopped
2 tsp sweet paprika
400 g/14 oz canned
    chopped tomatoes
2 tbsp tomato purée
2 carrots, sliced
2 tsp sugar
225 ml/8 fl oz red wine
5-cm/2-inch cinnamon stick
2 fresh rosemary sprigs
115 g/4 oz stoned black olives
2 tbsp lemon juice
2 tbsp chopped fresh mint
salt and pepper
fresh mint leaves, to garnish

method

1 Preheat the slow cooker, if necessary, or according to the manufacturer's instructions.

2 Spread out the flour on a plate and season with salt and pepper. Toss the lamb in the seasoned flour and shake off any excess. Heat the oil in a large, heavy-based saucepan. Add the lamb shanks and cook over a medium heat, turning frequently, for 6–8 minutes until browned all over. Transfer to a plate and set aside.

3 Add the onion and garlic to the saucepan and cook, stirring frequently, for 5 minutes until softened. Stir in the paprika and cook for 1 minute. Add the tomatoes, tomato purée, carrots, sugar, wine, cinnamon stick and rosemary and bring to the boil.

4 Transfer the vegetable mixture to the slow cooker and add the lamb shanks. Cover and cook on low for 8 hours until the lamb is very tender.

5 Add the olives, lemon juice and mint to the slow cooker. Re-cover and cook on high for 30 minutes. Remove and discard the rosemary and cinnamon and serve, garnished with mint leaves.

cinnamon lamb

ingredients

serves 6

2 tbsp plain flour
1 kg/2 lb 4 oz lean boneless
    lamb, cubed
2 tbsp olive oil
2 large onions, sliced
1 garlic clove, finely chopped
300 ml/10 fl oz red wine
2 tbsp red wine vinegar
400 g/14 oz canned
    chopped tomatoes
55 g/2 oz raisins
1 tbsp ground cinnamon
pinch of sugar
1 bay leaf
150 ml/5 fl oz Greek-style yogurt
2 garlic cloves, crushed
salt and pepper
paprika, for sprinkling

method

1 Preheat the slow cooker, if necessary, or according to the manufacturer's instructions.

2 Spread out the flour in a shallow dish and season with pepper. Add the lamb cubes and toss until well coated, shaking off any excess.

3 Heat the oil in a heavy-based frying pan. Add the onions and garlic and cook over a low heat, stirring occasionally, for 5 minutes until softened. Increase the heat to high, add the lamb and cook, stirring frequently, for 5 minutes until evenly browned.

4 Stir in the wine, vinegar and tomatoes with their can juices and bring to the boil, scraping up any sediment from the base of the pan. Transfer to the slow cooker, stir in the raisins, cinnamon, sugar and bay leaf and season with salt and pepper. Cover and cook on low for 8–8½ hours until the lamb is tender.

5 Meanwhile, prepare the topping. Mix together the yogurt and garlic in a small bowl and season to taste with salt and pepper. Cover and chill in the refrigerator until ready to serve.

6 Remove and discard the bay leaf. Serve each portion topped with a spoonful of the garlic-flavoured yogurt sprinkled with a little paprika.

pork with almonds

ingredients

serves 6

2 tbsp sunflower oil
2 onions, chopped
2 garlic cloves, finely chopped
5-cm/2-inch cinnamon stick
3 cloves
115 g/4 oz ground almonds
750 g/1 lb 10 oz boneless pork,
    cut into 2.5-cm/1-inch cubes
4 tomatoes, peeled and chopped
2 tbsp capers
115 g/4 oz green olives, stoned
3 pickled jalapeño chillies, drained,
    deseeded and cut into rings
350 ml/12 fl oz chicken stock
salt and pepper

method

1 Preheat the slow cooker, if necessary, or according to the manufacturer's instructions.

2 Heat half the oil in a large, heavy-based frying pan. Add the onions and cook over a low heat, stirring occasionally, for 5 minutes until softened. Add the garlic, cinnamon, cloves and almonds and cook, stirring frequently, for 8–10 minutes. Be careful not to burn the almonds.

3 Remove and discard the spices and transfer the almond mixture to a food processor. Process the mixture to a smooth purée.

4 Rinse out the pan and return to the heat. Heat the remaining oil, then add the pork, in batches if necessary. Cook over a medium heat, stirring frequently, for 5–10 minutes until browned all over. Return all the pork to the pan and add the almond purée, tomatoes, capers, olives, chillies and chicken stock. Bring to the boil, then transfer to the slow cooker.

5 Season with salt and pepper and mix well. Cover and cook on low for 5 hours. To serve, transfer to warmed plates and serve immediately.

pork & vegetable ragout

ingredients

serves 4

450 g/1 lb lean, boneless pork
1½ tbsp plain flour
1 tsp ground coriander
1 tsp ground cumin
1½ tsp ground cinnamon
1 tbsp olive oil
1 onion, chopped
400 g/14 oz canned
    chopped tomatoes
2 tbsp tomato purée
300 ml/10 fl oz chicken stock
225 g/8 oz carrots, chopped
350 g/12 oz squash, such as
    kabocha, peeled, deseeded
    and chopped
225 g/8 oz leeks, sliced, blanched
    and drained
115 g/4 oz okra, trimmed
    and sliced
salt and pepper
sprigs of fresh parsley, to garnish
couscous, to serve

method

1 Preheat the slow cooker, if necessary, or according to the manufacturer's instructions.

2 Trim off any visible fat from the pork and cut the meat into thin strips about 5 cm/2 inches long. Mix together the flour, coriander, cumin and cinnamon in a shallow dish, add the pork strips and toss well to coat. Shake off the excess and reserve the remaining spiced flour.

3 Heat the oil in a heavy-based frying pan. Add the onion and cook over a low heat, stirring occasionally, for 5 minutes until softened. Add the pork strips, increase the heat to high and cook, stirring frequently, for 5 minutes until browned all over. Sprinkle in the reserved spiced flour and cook, stirring constantly, for 2 minutes, then remove the pan from the heat.

4 Gradually stir in the tomatoes with their can juices. Combine the tomato purée with the stock in a jug, then gradually stir the mixture into the frying pan. Add the carrots, return the pan to the heat and bring to the boil, stirring constantly.

5 Transfer to the slow cooker, stir in the squash, leeks and okra, and season with salt and pepper. Cover and cook on low for 5–6 hours until the meat and vegetables are tender. Garnish with parsley sprigs and serve with couscous.

spicy pulled pork

ingredients

serves 4

2 onions, sliced
1.5 kg/3 lb 5 oz boned
   and rolled pork shoulder
2 tbsp demerara sugar
2 tbsp Worcestershire sauce
1 tbsp American mustard
2 tbsp tomato ketchup
1 tbsp cider vinegar
salt and pepper
hamburger buns or ciabatta
   rolls, to serve

method

1 Preheat the slow cooker, if necessary, or according to the manufacturer's instructions.

2 Put the onions in the slow cooker and place the pork on top. Mix the sugar, Worcestershire sauce, mustard, ketchup and vinegar together and spread all over the surface of the pork. Season to taste with salt and pepper. Cover and cook on low for 8 hours.

3 Remove the pork from the slow cooker and use 2 forks to pull it apart into shreds.

4 Skim any excess fat from the juices and stir a little juice into the pork. Serve in hamburger buns, with the remaining juices for spooning over the pork.

maple-glazed pork ribs

ingredients

serves 4

1 onion, finely chopped
2 plum tomatoes, diced
3 tbsp maple syrup
2 tbsp soy sauce
2 tsp hot chilli sauce
1.5 kg/3 lb 5 oz meaty pork ribs,
    cut into single ribs
salt and pepper

method

1 Preheat the slow cooker, if necessary, or according to the manufacturer's instructions.

2 Combine the onion, tomatoes, maple syrup, soy sauce, chilli sauce, and salt and pepper to taste in a large bowl. Add the pork ribs and turn to coat evenly.

3 Arrange the ribs in the slow cooker, cover and cook on high for 4 hours. If possible, turn the ribs halfway through the cooking time.

4 Lift out the ribs and place on a warmed platter. Skim the excess fat from the juices and spoon the juices over the ribs to serve.

slow roast chicken

ingredients

serves 4-6

1.5 kg/3 lb 5 oz
   oven-ready chicken
½ lemon
1 tbsp olive oil
½ tsp dried thyme
½ tsp paprika
salt and pepper

method

1 Preheat the slow cooker, if necessary, or according to the manufacturer's instructions.

2 Wipe the chicken with absorbent kitchen paper and tuck the ½ lemon inside the body cavity. Brush the oil over the chicken skin and sprinkle with thyme, paprika and salt and pepper, rubbing in with your fingers to cover all the skin.

3 Place the chicken in the slow cooker, cover and cook on high for 3 hours. Reduce the heat to low and cook for a further 4 hours, until the chicken is tender and the juices run clear when a skewer is inserted into the thickest part of the meat.

4 Carefully remove the chicken and place on a warmed platter, then skim any fat from the juices. Adjust the seasoning to taste and serve.

nutty chicken

ingredients

serves 4

3 tbsp sunflower oil
4 skinless chicken portions
2 shallots, chopped
1 tsp ground ginger
1 tbsp plain flour
425 ml/15 fl oz beef stock
55 g/2 oz walnut pieces
grated rind of 1 lemon
2 tbsp lemon juice
1 tbsp black treacle
salt and pepper
sprigs of fresh watercress,
     to garnish

method

1 Preheat the slow cooker, if necessary, or according to the manufacturer's instructions.

2 Heat the oil in a large, heavy-based frying pan. Season the chicken portions with salt and pepper and add to the pan. Cook the chicken over a medium heat, turning occasionally, for 5–8 minutes until lightly golden all over. Transfer to the slow cooker.

3 Add the shallots to the pan and cook, stirring occasionally, for 3–4 minutes until softened. Sprinkle in the ginger and flour and cook, stirring constantly, for 1 minute. Gradually stir in the stock and bring to the boil, stirring constantly. Lower the heat and simmer for 1 minute, then stir in the nuts, lemon rind and juice and treacle.

4 Pour the sauce over the chicken. Cover and cook on low for 6 hours until the chicken is cooked through and tender. Taste and adjust the seasoning if necessary. Transfer the chicken to warmed bowls, spoon some of the sauce over each portion, garnish with watercress sprigs and serve immediately.

chicken cacciatore

ingredients

serves 4

3 tbsp olive oil
4 skinless chicken portions
2 onions, sliced
2 garlic cloves, finely chopped
400 g/14 oz canned
    chopped tomatoes
1 tbsp tomato purée
2 tbsp chopped fresh parsley
2 tsp fresh thyme leaves
150 ml/5 fl oz red wine
salt and pepper
sprigs of fresh thyme, to garnish

method

1 Preheat the slow cooker, if necessary, or according to the manufacturer's instructions.

2 Heat the oil in a heavy-based frying pan. Add the chicken portions and cook over a medium heat, turning occasionally, for 10 minutes until golden all over. Using a slotted spoon, transfer the chicken to the slow cooker.

3 Add the onions to the pan and cook, stirring occasionally, for 5 minutes until softened and just turning golden. Add the garlic, tomatoes and their can juices, tomato purée, parsley, thyme and wine. Season with salt and pepper and bring to the boil.

4 Pour the tomato mixture over the chicken pieces. Cover and cook on low for 5 hours until the chicken is tender and cooked through. Taste and adjust the seasoning if necessary and serve, garnished with sprigs of thyme.

chicken in riesling

ingredients

serves 4–6

2 tbsp plain flour
1 chicken, about 1.6 kg/3 lb 8 oz,
    cut into 8 pieces
55 g/2 oz unsalted butter
1 tbsp sunflower oil
4 shallots, finely chopped
12 button mushrooms, sliced
2 tbsp brandy
500 ml/18 fl oz Riesling wine
250 ml/9 fl oz double cream
salt and pepper
chopped fresh flat-leaf parsley,
    to garnish

method

1 Preheat the slow cooker, if necessary, or according to the manufacturer's instructions.

2 Put the flour in a shallow dish and season with salt and pepper. Toss the chicken pieces in the flour until well coated. Heat half the butter with the oil in a heavy-based frying pan. Add the chicken pieces and cook over a medium–high heat, turning frequently, for 10 minutes until golden all over. Transfer them to a plate.

3 Melt the remaining butter in the frying pan. Add the shallots and mushrooms and cook over a medium–high heat, stirring constantly, for 3 minutes until lightly browned. Return the chicken to the frying pan and remove it from the heat. Warm the brandy in a small ladle, ignite and pour it over the chicken, shaking the pan gently until the flames have died down.

4 Return the pan to the heat and pour in the wine. Bring to the boil over a low heat. Transfer to the slow cooker, cover and cook on low for 5–6 hours until the chicken is tender. Transfer the chicken to a serving dish and keep warm. Skim off any fat and pour the liquid into a saucepan. Stir in the cream and bring just to the boil over a low heat. Season to taste with salt and pepper and pour the sauce over the chicken. Sprinkle with chopped parsley and serve immediately.

barbecue chicken

ingredients

serves 4

8 skinless chicken drumsticks
  or thighs
3 tbsp tomato purée
2 tbsp clear honey
1 tbsp Worcestershire sauce
juice of ½ lemon
½ tsp crushed dried chillies
1 garlic clove, crushed
salt and pepper

method

1 Preheat the slow cooker, if necessary, or according to the manufacturer's instructions.

2 Using a sharp knife, cut slashes into the thickest parts of the chicken flesh.

3 Mix the tomato purée, honey, Worcestershire sauce, lemon juice, chillies and garlic together and season with salt and pepper. Add the chicken and toss well to coat evenly.

4 Arrange the chicken in the slow cooker, cover and cook on high for 3 hours.

5 Remove the chicken with a draining spoon. Skim any fat from the juices and spoon over the chicken to serve.

variation

Use a whole chicken if preferred. Clean the chicken inside and out with kitchen paper. Fry the chicken in butter in a large saucepan until brown all over. Brush the sauce over the chicken. Place in the slow cooker and cook on high for 3 hours.

seafood in saffron sauce

ingredients

serves 4

2 tbsp olive oil
1 onion, sliced
2 celery sticks, sliced
pinch of saffron threads
1 tbsp chopped fresh thyme
2 garlic cloves, finely chopped
800 g/1 lb 12 oz canned tomatoes,
    drained and chopped
175 ml/6 fl oz dry white wine
2 litres/3½ pints fish stock
225 g/8 oz live clams
225 g/8 oz live mussels
350 g/12 oz red mullet fillets
450 g/1 lb monkfish fillet
225 g/8 oz squid rings,
    thawed if frozen
2 tbsp shredded fresh basil leaves
salt and pepper

method

1 Preheat the slow cooker, if necessary, or according to the manufacturer's instructions.

2 Heat the oil in a large heavy-based saucepan. Add the onion, celery, saffron, thyme and a pinch of salt and cook over a low heat, stirring occasionally, for 5 minutes until softened. Add the garlic and cook, stirring constantly, for 2 minutes.

3 Add the tomatoes, wine and stock, season with salt and pepper and bring to the boil, stirring constantly. Transfer the mixture to the slow cooker, cover and cook on low for 5 hours.

4 Meanwhile, scrub the shellfish under cold running water and pull the 'beards' off the mussels. Discard any with broken shells or that do not shut immediately when sharply tapped. Cut the mullet and monkfish fillets into bite-sized chunks.

5 Add the pieces of fish, the shellfish and the squid rings to the slow cooker, re-cover and cook on high for 30 minutes until the clams and mussels have opened and the fish is cooked through. Discard any shellfish that remain closed. Stir in the basil and serve.

mixed mediterranean shellfish

ingredients

serves 8

1 tbsp olive oil
115 g/4 oz bacon, diced
2 tbsp butter
2 shallots, chopped
2 leeks, sliced
2 celery sticks, chopped
2 potatoes, diced
675 g/1 lb 8 oz tomatoes, peeled, deseeded and chopped
3 tbsp chopped fresh parsley
3 tbsp snipped fresh chives, plus extra to garnish
1 bay leaf
1 fresh thyme sprig
1.4 litres/2½ pints fish stock
24 live mussels
24 live clams
450 g/1 lb sea bream fillets
24 raw tiger prawns
salt and pepper

method

1 Preheat the slow cooker, if necessary, or according to the manufacturer's instructions.

2 Heat the oil in a heavy-based frying pan. Add the bacon and cook, stirring frequently, for 5–8 minutes until crisp. Using a slotted spoon, transfer to the slow cooker. Add the butter to the frying pan and when it has melted, add the shallots, leeks, celery and potatoes. Cook over a low heat, stirring occasionally, for 5 minutes until softened. Stir in the tomatoes, parsley, chives, bay leaf and thyme, pour in the stock and bring to the boil, stirring constantly. Pour the mixture into the slow cooker, cover and cook on low for 7 hours.

3 Meanwhile, scrub the mussels and clams under cold running water and pull off the 'beards' from the mussels. Discard any with broken shells or that do not shut immediately when sharply tapped. Cut the fish fillets into bite-size chunks. Peel and devein the prawns.

4 Remove and discard the bay leaf and thyme sprig from the stew. Season with salt and pepper and add all the fish and seafood. Re-cover and cook on high for 30 minutes. Discard any shellfish that remain closed. Serve garnished with extra chives.

french-style fish stew

ingredients

serves 4–6

1 prepared squid
900 g/2 lb mixed white fish,
  such as sea bass, monkfish,
  red mullet and grouper, filleted,
  and cut into chunks
24 large raw prawns, peeled and
  deveined, reserving heads and
  shells tied in muslin
2 tbsp olive oil
1 large onion, finely chopped
1 fennel bulb, thinly sliced,
  feathery fronds reserved
2 large garlic cloves, crushed
4 tbsp Pernod
large pinch of saffron threads,
  freshly toasted
1 litre/1¾ pints fish stock
2 large tomatoes, peeled, deseeded
  and diced, or 400 g/14 oz
  canned chopped tomatoes,
  drained
1 tbsp tomato purée
1 bay leaf
pinch of sugar
pinch of dried chilli flakes
  (optional)
salt and pepper

method

1 Preheat the slow cooker, if necessary, or according to the manufacturer's instructions.

2 Cut off and reserve the tentacles from the squid and slice the body into 5-mm/¼-inch rings. Place the seafood in a bowl, cover and chill in the refrigerator until required.

3 Heat the oil in a heavy-based frying pan. Add the onion and fennel and cook over a low heat, stirring occasionally, for 5 minutes until softened. Add the garlic and cook, stirring frequently, for 2 minutes. Remove the pan from the heat. Heat the Pernod in a ladle or small saucepan, ignite and pour it over the onion and fennel, gently shaking the frying pan until the flames have died down.

4 Return the frying pan to the heat, stir in the toasted saffron, stock, tomatoes, tomato purée, bay leaf, sugar and chilli flakes, if using, and season with salt and pepper. Bring to the boil, then transfer to the slow cooker, add the bag of prawn shells, cover and cook on low for 6 hours.

5 Remove and discard the bag of prawn shells and the bay leaf. Add the fish and seafood to the slow cooker, cover and cook on high for 30 minutes. Serve garnished with the reserved fennel fronds.

pollock bake

ingredients

serves 4

1 tbsp olive oil
1 red onion, sliced
1 yellow pepper, deseeded
    and sliced
4 pollock fillets, about
    140 g/5 oz each
2 tomatoes, thinly sliced
8 stoned black olives, halved
1 garlic clove, thinly sliced
2 tsp balsamic vinegar
juice of 1 orange
salt and pepper

method

1 Preheat the slow cooker, if necessary, or according to the manufacturer's instructions.

2 Heat the oil in a frying pan, add the onion and yellow pepper and fry over a high heat for 3–4 minutes, stirring, until lightly browned. Transfer to the slow cooker, cover and cook on high for 1 hour.

3 Arrange the fish fillets over the vegetables and season with salt and pepper. Arrange a layer of tomatoes and olives over the top and sprinkle with the garlic, vinegar and salt and pepper. Pour over the orange juice, cover and cook on high for a further 1 hour. Serve immediately.

poached salmon with dill & lime

ingredients

serves 4

30 g/1 oz butter, melted
1 onion, thinly sliced
450 g/1 lb potatoes, peeled
    and thinly sliced
100 ml/3½ fl oz hot fish stock
    or water
4 pieces skinless salmon fillet,
    about 140 g/5 oz each
juice of 1 lime
2 tbsp chopped fresh dill
salt and pepper
lime wedges, to serve

method

1 Preheat the slow cooker, if necessary, or according to the manufacturer's instructions.

2 Brush the base of the slow cooker with 1 tablespoon of the butter. Layer the onion and potatoes in the slow cooker, sprinkling with salt and pepper between the layers. Add the stock and dot with 1 tablespoon of the butter. Cover and cook on low for 3 hours.

3 Arrange the salmon over the vegetables in a single layer. Drizzle the lime juice over, sprinkle with dill and salt and pepper and pour the remaining butter on top. Cover and cook on low for a further 1 hour, until the fish flakes easily.

4 Serve the salmon and vegetables on warmed plates with the juices spooned over and lime wedges on the side.

baked asparagus & spinach risotto

ingredients

serves 4

2 tbsp olive oil
4 shallots, finely chopped
280 g/10 oz arborio rice
1 garlic clove, crushed
100 ml/3½ fl oz dry white wine
850 ml/1½ pints hot chicken stock
 or vegetable stock
200 g/7 oz asparagus spears
200 g/7 oz baby spinach leaves
40 g/1½ oz finely grated
 Parmesan cheese
salt and pepper

method

1 Preheat the slow cooker, if necessary, or according to the manufacturer's instructions.

2 Heat the oil in a frying pan, add the shallots and fry over a medium heat, stirring, for 2–3 minutes. Add the rice and garlic and cook for a further 2 minutes, stirring. Add the wine and allow it to boil for 30 seconds.

3 Transfer the rice mixture to the slow cooker, add the stock and season to taste with salt and pepper. Cover and cook on high for 2 hours, or until most of the liquid is absorbed.

4 Cut the asparagus into 4.5-cm/1¾-inch lengths. Stir into the rice, then spread the spinach over the top. Replace the lid and cook on high for a further 30 minutes, until the asparagus is just tender and the spinach is wilted.

5 Stir in the spinach with the Parmesan cheese, then adjust the seasoning to taste and serve immediately in warmed bowls.

tuscan beans

ingredients

serves 4

1 large fennel bulb
2 tbsp olive oil
1 red onion, cut into small wedges
2–4 garlic cloves, sliced
1 green chilli, deseeded
    and chopped
1 aubergine, about 225 g/8 oz,
    cut into chunks
2 tbsp tomato purée
450 ml/16 fl oz vegetable stock
450 g/1 lb tomatoes, sliced
1 tbsp balsamic vinegar
4 fresh oregano sprigs
400 g/14 oz canned borlotti
    beans, drained and rinsed
400 g/14 oz canned flageolet
    beans, drained and rinsed
1 yellow pepper, deseeded and cut
    into small strips
1 courgette, halved lengthways
    and sliced
55 g/2 oz stoned black olives
salt and pepper
25 g/1 oz Parmesan cheese,
    to garnish

method

1 Preheat the slow cooker, if necessary, or according to the manufacturer's instructions.

2 Trim the fennel bulb, reserving the feathery fronds, then cut the bulb into thin strips. Heat the oil in a heavy-based frying pan. Add the fennel strips, onion, garlic and chilli and cook over a low heat, stirring occasionally, for 5–8 minutes until softened. Add the aubergine and cook, stirring frequently, for 5 minutes.

3 Mix together the tomato purée and half the stock in a jug and add to the frying pan. Pour in the remaining stock, add the tomatoes, vinegar and oregano and bring to the boil, stirring constantly.

4 Transfer the mixture to the slow cooker. Stir in the beans, yellow pepper, courgette and olives and season with salt and pepper. Cover and cook on high for 3–4 hours, until all the vegetables are tender.

5 Taste and adjust the seasoning if necessary. Thinly shave the Parmesan over the top of the stew, garnish with the reserved fennel fronds and serve.

mixed bean chilli

ingredients

serves 4–6

2 tbsp sunflower oil
1 onion, chopped
1 garlic clove, finely chopped
1 fresh red chilli, deseeded
    and chopped
1 yellow pepper, deseeded
    and chopped
1 tsp ground cumin
1 tbsp chilli powder
115 g/4 oz dried red kidney beans,
    soaked in water overnight, or
    for at least 5 hours
115 g/4 oz dried black beans,
    soaked in water overnight, or
    for at least 5 hours
115 g/4 oz dried pinto beans,
    soaked in water overnight, or
    for at least 5 hours
1 litre/1¾ pints vegetable stock
1 tbsp sugar
salt and pepper
chopped fresh coriander,
    to garnish

method

1 Preheat the slow cooker, if necessary, or according to the manufacturer's instructions.

2 Heat the oil in a large, heavy-based saucepan. Add the onion, garlic, chilli and yellow pepper and cook over a medium heat, stirring occasionally, for 5 minutes. Stir in the cumin and chilli powder and cook, stirring, for 1–2 minutes. Add the drained beans and stock and bring to the boil. Boil vigorously for 15 minutes.

3 Transfer the mixture to the slow cooker, cover and cook on low for 10 hours until the beans are tender.

4 Season the mixture with salt and pepper, then ladle about one-third into a bowl. Mash well with a potato masher, then return the mashed beans to the slow cooker and stir in the sugar. Serve immediately, sprinkled with chopped fresh coriander.

mixed vegetables

ingredients

serves 4

500 g/1 lb 2 oz potatoes,
    peeled and cubed
2 courgettes, cubed
2 red peppers, deseeded
    and cubed
2 red onions, sliced
2 tsp mixed dried herbs
250 ml/9 fl oz hot vegetable stock
salt and pepper

method

1 Preheat the slow cooker, if necessary, or according
  to the manufacturer's instructions.

2 Layer all the vegetables in the slow cooker, sprinkling
  with herbs and salt and pepper between the layers.

3 Pour over the stock. Cover and cook on low for 7 hours.
  Serve in warmed bowls.

around the world

brunswick chicken

ingredients

serves 6

1.8 kg/4 lb chicken portions
2 tbsp paprika
2 tbsp olive oil
2 tbsp butter
450 g/1 lb onions, chopped
2 yellow peppers, deseeded
    and chopped
400 g/14 oz canned chopped
    tomatoes
225 ml/8 fl oz dry white wine
450 ml/16 fl oz chicken stock
1 tbsp Worcestershire sauce
1/2 tsp Tabasco sauce
1 tbsp finely chopped fresh parsley
2 tbsp plain flour
325 g/11 1/2 oz canned sweetcorn
    kernels, drained
425 g/15 oz canned butter beans,
    drained and rinsed
salt
sprigs of fresh parsley, to garnish

method

1 Preheat the slow cooker, if necessary, or according to the manufacturer's instructions.

2 Season the chicken portions with salt and dust with the paprika. Heat the oil and butter in a heavy-based frying pan. Add the chicken portions and cook over a medium–high heat, turning frequently, for 10 minutes until golden brown all over. Using a slotted spoon, transfer the chicken to the slow cooker.

3 Add the onions and peppers to the frying pan, lower the heat and cook, stirring occasionally, for 5 minutes until softened. Add the tomatoes with their can juices, wine, stock, Worcestershire sauce, Tabasco sauce and chopped parsley and bring to the boil, stirring constantly. Pour the mixture over the chicken, cover and cook on low for 5 hours.

4 Mix the flour with 4 tablespoons of water to a paste in a small, heatproof bowl. Add a ladleful of the cooking liquid and mix well, then stir the mixture into the stew. Add the sweetcorn and butter beans, re-cover and cook on high for 30 minutes until the chicken is tender and cooked through. Serve garnished with parsley sprigs.

chipotle chicken

ingredients

serves 4

4–6 dried chipotle chillies
4 garlic cloves, unpeeled
1 small onion, chopped
400 g/14 oz canned
    chopped tomatoes
300 ml/10 fl oz hot chicken
    or vegetable stock
4 skinless chicken breasts
salt and pepper
chopped fresh flat-leaf parsley,
    to garnish

method.

1 Preheat the oven to 200°C/400°F/Gas Mark 6. Place the chillies in a bowl and pour in just enough hot water to cover. Set aside to soak for 30 minutes. Meanwhile, place the unpeeled garlic cloves on a baking sheet and roast in the oven for about 10 minutes until soft. Remove from the oven and set aside to cool.

2 Drain the chillies, reserving 125 ml/4 fl oz of the soaking water. Deseed the chillies, if you like, and chop coarsely. Place the chillies and reserved soaking water in a blender or food processor and process to a purée. Peel and mash the garlic in a bowl.

3 Preheat the slow cooker, if necessary, or according to the manufacturer's instructions.

4 Place the chilli purée, garlic, onion and tomatoes in the slow cooker and stir in the stock. Season the chicken portions with salt and pepper and place them in the slow cooker. Cover and cook on low for about 5 hours until the chicken is tender and cooked through.

5 Lift the chicken out of the slow cooker with a slotted spoon, cover and keep warm. Pour the cooking liquid into a saucepan and bring to the boil on the hob. Boil for 5–10 minutes until reduced. Place the chicken on warmed plates, spoon the sauce over it, garnish with the chopped parsley and serve.

florida chicken

ingredients

serves 4

1½ tbsp plain flour
450 g/1 lb skinless, boneless
   chicken, cut into bite-sized
   pieces
1 tbsp olive oil
1 onion, cut into wedges
2 celery sticks, sliced
150 ml/5 fl oz orange juice
300 ml/10 fl oz chicken stock
1 tbsp light soy sauce
1–2 tsp clear honey
1 tbsp grated orange rind
1 orange pepper, deseeded
   and chopped
225 g/8 oz courgettes, halved
   lengthways and sliced
2 corn on the cobs, cut into chunks
1 orange, peeled and segmented
salt and pepper
1 tbsp chopped fresh parsley,
   to garnish

method

1 Preheat the slow cooker, if necessary, or according
   to the manufacturer's instructions.

2 Spread out the flour in a shallow dish and season with
   salt and pepper. Add the chicken and toss well to coat,
   shaking off any excess. Reserve the remaining
   seasoned flour.

3 Heat the oil in a heavy-based frying pan. Add the
   chicken and cook over a high heat, stirring frequently,
   for 5 minutes until golden brown all over. Using a
   slotted spoon, transfer the chicken to the slow cooker.

4 Add the onion and celery to the frying pan, lower the
   heat and cook, stirring occasionally, for 5 minutes until
   softened. Sprinkle in the reserved seasoned flour and
   cook, stirring constantly, for 2 minutes. Remove the
   pan from the heat. Gradually stir in the orange juice,
   stock, soy sauce and honey, then add the orange rind.
   Return the pan to the heat and bring to the boil,
   stirring constantly.

5 Pour the mixture over the chicken and add the orange
   pepper, courgettes and corn on the cobs. Cover and
   cook on low for 5 hours until the chicken is tender and
   cooked through. Stir in the orange segments, re-cover
   and cook on high for 15 minutes. Serve garnished with
   the parsley.

chicken italian-style

ingredients

serves 4

1 tbsp plain flour
4 chicken portions, about
    175 g/6 oz each
2½ tbsp olive oil
8–12 shallots, halved if large
2–4 garlic cloves, sliced
400 ml/14 fl oz chicken stock
50 ml/2 fl oz dry sherry
4 fresh thyme sprigs
115 g/4 oz cherry tomatoes
115 g/4 oz baby sweetcorn,
    halved lengthways
2 slices white or wholemeal bread,
    crusts removed, cubed
salt and pepper
1 tbsp chopped fresh thyme,
    to garnish

method

1 Preheat the slow cooker, if necessary, or according to the manufacturer's instructions.

2 Spread out the flour in a shallow dish and season with salt and pepper. Add the chicken portions and toss well to coat, shaking off any excess. Reserve the remaining seasoned flour. Heat 1 tablespoon of the oil in a heavy-based frying pan. Add the chicken portions and cook over a medium–high heat, turning frequently, for 10 minutes until golden brown all over. Using a slotted spoon, transfer the chicken to the slow cooker.

3 Add the shallots and garlic to the frying pan, lower the heat and cook, stirring occasionally, for 5 minutes until softened. Sprinkle in the reserved seasoned flour and cook, stirring constantly, for 2 minutes. Remove from the heat and gradually stir in the stock and sherry, then bring to the boil, stirring constantly. Pour the mixture over the chicken and add the thyme sprigs, tomatoes and baby sweetcorn. Cover and cook on low for 5–6 hours until the chicken is tender and cooked through.

4 Meanwhile, heat the remaining oil in a frying pan, add the bread cubes and cook, stirring frequently, for 4–5 minutes until golden all over. Remove and discard the thyme sprigs from the stew, then serve, garnished with the croûtons and chopped thyme.

bulgarian chicken

ingredients

serves 6

4 tbsp sunflower oil
6 chicken portions
2 onions, chopped
2 garlic cloves, finely chopped
1 fresh red chilli, deseeded and
    finely chopped
6 tomatoes, peeled and chopped
2 tsp sweet paprika
1 bay leaf
225 ml/8 fl oz hot chicken stock
salt and pepper

method

1 Preheat the slow cooker, if necessary, or according to the manufacturer's instructions.

2 Heat the oil in a large, heavy-based frying pan. Add the chicken portions and cook over a medium heat, turning occasionally, for about 10 minutes, until golden all over.

3 Transfer the contents of the pan to the slow cooker and add the onions, garlic, chilli and tomatoes. Sprinkle in the paprika, add the bay leaf and pour in the stock. Season with salt and pepper. Stir well, cover and cook on low for 6 hours until the chicken is cooked through and tender. Remove and discard the bay leaf, then serve immediately.

easy chinese chicken

ingredients

serves 4

2 tsp grated fresh ginger
4 garlic cloves, finely chopped
2 star anise
150 ml/5 fl oz Chinese rice wine
   or medium dry sherry
2 tbsp dark soy sauce
1 tsp sesame oil
4 skinless chicken thighs or
   drumsticks
shredded spring onions, to garnish
boiled rice, to serve

method

1 Preheat the slow cooker, if necessary, or according to the manufacturer's instructions.

2 Mix together the ginger, garlic, star anise, rice wine, soy sauce and sesame oil in a bowl and stir in 5 tablespoons of water. Place the chicken in a saucepan, add the spice mixture and bring to the boil.

3 Transfer the mixture to the slow cooker, cover and cook on low for 4 hours or until the chicken is tender and cooked through.

4 Remove and discard the star anise. Transfer the chicken to warmed plates and serve garnished with shredded spring onions with boiled rice.

jambalaya-style duckling

ingredients

serves 4

4 duckling breasts, about
175 g/6 oz each
2 tbsp olive oil
225 g/8 oz gammon,
cut into small chunks
225 g/8 oz chorizo or other spicy
sausages, skinned and sliced
1 onion, chopped
3 garlic cloves, chopped
3 celery sticks, chopped
1–2 red chillies, deseeded
and chopped
1 green pepper, deseeded
and chopped
600 ml/1 pint chicken stock
1 tbsp chopped fresh oregano
400 g/14 oz canned chopped
tomatoes
1–2 tsp hot pepper sauce
fresh parsley sprigs, to garnish
green salad and boiled rice,
to serve

method

1 Preheat the slow cooker, if necessary, or according to the manufacturer's instructions.

2 Remove and discard the skin and any visible fat from the duckling breasts and cut the flesh into bite-sized pieces. Heat half the oil in a heavy-based frying pan, add the duckling, gammon and chorizo and cook over a high heat, stirring frequently, for 5 minutes until browned all over. Using a slotted spoon, transfer the meat to the slow cooker.

3 Add the onion, garlic, celery and chilli to the frying pan, lower the heat and cook, stirring occasionally, for 5 minutes until softened. Add the green pepper and stir in the stock, oregano, tomatoes with the can juices and hot pepper sauce. Bring to the boil, then pour the mixture over the meat.

4 Cover the slow cooker and cook the jambalaya on low for 6 hours, until the meat is tender. Serve garnished with parsley sprigs and accompanied by a green salad and boiled rice.

mexican pork chops

ingredients

serves 4

4 pork chops, trimmed of excess fat
2 tbsp sunflower oil
450 g/1 lb canned pineapple
    cubes in fruit juice
1 red pepper, deseeded
    and finely chopped
2 fresh jalapeño chillies,
    deseeded and finely chopped
1 onion, finely chopped
1 tbsp chopped fresh coriander
125 ml/4 fl oz hot chicken stock
salt and pepper
sprigs of fresh coriander,
    to garnish
tortillas, to serve

method

1 Preheat the slow cooker, if necessary, or according to the manufacturer's instructions.

2 Season the chops with salt and pepper. Heat the oil in a large, heavy-based frying pan. Add the chops and cook over a medium heat for 2–3 minutes each side until lightly browned. Transfer them to the slow cooker. Drain the pineapple, reserving the juice, and set aside.

3 Add the red pepper, chillies and onion to the frying pan and cook, stirring occasionally, for 5 minutes until the onion is softened. Transfer the mixture to the slow cooker and add the coriander and stock, together with 125 ml/4 fl oz of the reserved pineapple juice. Cover and cook on low for 6 hours until the chops are tender.

4 Add the reserved pineapple to the slow cooker, re-cover and cook on high for 15 minutes. Garnish with fresh coriander sprigs and serve immediately, with tortillas.

poor man's cassoulet

ingredients

serves 4

2 tbsp sunflower oil
2 onions, chopped
2 garlic cloves, finely chopped
115 g/4 oz streaky bacon,
    derinded and chopped
500 g/1 lb 2 oz pork sausages
400 g/14 oz canned haricot,
    red kidney or black-eyed
    beans, drained and rinsed
2 tbsp chopped fresh parsley
150 ml/5 fl oz hot beef stock
4 slices French bread and
    55 g/2 oz grated Gruyère
    cheese, to serve

method

1 Preheat the slow cooker, if necessary, or according to the manufacturer's instructions.

2 Heat the oil in a heavy-based frying pan. Add the onions and cook over a low heat, stirring occasionally, for 5 minutes until softened. Add the garlic, bacon and sausages and cook, stirring and turning the sausages occasionally, for a further 5 minutes.

3 Using a slotted spoon, transfer the mixture from the frying pan to the slow cooker. Add the beans, parsley and beef stock, then cover and cook on low for 6 hours.

4 Preheat the grill to high. Just before serving, lightly toast the bread under the grill. Divide the grated cheese between the toast slices and place under the grill until just melted.

5 Ladle the stew onto warmed plates, top each portion with the cheese-toast and serve.

jambalaya

ingredients

serves 6

½ tsp cayenne pepper
½ tsp freshly ground
    black pepper
1 tsp salt
2 tsp chopped fresh thyme
350 g/12 oz skinless, boneless
    chicken breasts, diced
2 tbsp sunflower oil
2 onions, chopped
2 garlic cloves, finely chopped
2 green peppers, deseeded
    and chopped
2 celery sticks, chopped
115 g/4 oz smoked ham, chopped
175 g/6 oz chorizo sausage,
    skinned and sliced
400 g/14 oz canned
    chopped tomatoes
2 tbsp tomato purée
225 ml/8 fl oz chicken stock
450 g/1 lb peeled raw prawns
450 g/1 lb cooked rice
snipped fresh chives, to garnish

method

1 Preheat the slow cooker, if necessary, or according to the manufacturer's instructions.

2 Mix together the cayenne, black pepper, salt and thyme in a bowl. Add the chicken and toss to coat. Heat the oil in a large, heavy-based saucepan. Add the onions, garlic, green peppers and celery and cook over a low heat, stirring occasionally, for 5 minutes. Add the chicken and cook over a medium heat, stirring frequently, for a further 5 minutes until golden all over. Stir in the ham, chorizo, tomatoes, tomato purée and stock and bring to the boil.

3 Transfer the mixture to the slow cooker. Cover and cook on low for 6 hours. Add the prawns and rice, re-cover and cook on high for 30 minutes.

4 Taste and adjust the seasoning, if necessary. Transfer to warm plates, garnish with chives and serve the jambalaya immediately.

oriental pork

ingredients

serves 4

450 g/1 lb lean boneless pork
1½ tbsp plain flour
1–2 tbsp groundnut oil
1 onion, cut into small wedges
2–3 garlic cloves, chopped
2.5-cm/1-inch piece fresh ginger,
    grated
1 red pepper, deseeded and sliced
1 green pepper, deseeded
    and sliced
1 tbsp tomato purée
300 ml/10 fl oz chicken stock
225 g/8 oz canned pineapple
    chunks in natural juice
1–1½ tbsp dark soy sauce
1½ tbsp rice vinegar
4 spring onions, diagonally sliced,
    to garnish
rice, to serve

method

1 Preheat the slow cooker, if necessary, or according to the manufacturer's instructions.

2 Trim off all visible fat from the pork and cut the meat into 2.5-cm/1-inch chunks. Spread out the flour in a shallow dish, add the pork and toss well to coat, shaking off any excess. Reserve the remaining flour.

3 Heat the oil in a heavy-based frying pan. Add the onion, garlic, ginger and peppers and cook over a low heat, stirring occasionally, for 5 minutes until softened. Add the pork, increase the heat and cook, stirring frequently, for 5 minutes until browned all over. Sprinkle in the reserved flour and cook, stirring constantly, for 2 minutes, then remove the pan from the heat.

4 Mix the tomato purée and stock in a jug, then gradually stir into the frying pan. Drain the pineapple, reserving the juice. Stir the juice and soy sauce into the pan. Return the pan to the heat and bring to the boil, stirring constantly. Transfer to the slow cooker, cover and cook on low for 5–6 hours.

5 Stir in the pineapple and vinegar, re-cover and cook on high for 30 minutes. Garnish with the sliced spring onions and serve with rice.

neapolitan beef

ingredients

serves 6

300 ml/10 fl oz red wine
4 tbsp olive oil
1 celery stick, chopped
2 shallots, sliced
4 garlic cloves, finely chopped
1 bay leaf
10 fresh basil leaves, plus extra
    to garnish
3 fresh parsley sprigs
pinch of grated nutmeg
pinch of ground cinnamon
2 cloves
1.5 kg/3 lb 5 oz beef silverside
1–2 garlic cloves, thinly sliced
55 g/2 oz streaky bacon or
    pancetta, derinded and
    chopped
400g/14 oz canned chopped
    tomatoes
2 tbsp tomato purée

method

1 Preheat the slow cooker, if necessary, or according to the manufacturer's instructions.

2 Combine the wine, 2 tablespoons of the olive oil, the celery, shallots, garlic, herbs and spices in a large, non-metallic bowl. Add the beef, cover and marinate, turning occasionally, for 12 hours.

3 Drain the beef, reserving the marinade, and pat dry with kitchen paper. Make small incisions all over the beef using a sharp knife. Insert a slice of garlic and a piece of bacon in each 'pocket'. Heat the remaining oil in a large frying pan. Add the meat and cook over a medium heat, turning frequently, until browned all over. Transfer to the slow cooker.

4 Strain the reserved marinade into the frying pan and bring to the boil. Stir in the tomatoes and tomato purée. Stir well, then pour the mixture over the beef. Cover and cook on low for about 9 hours until tender. If possible, turn the beef over halfway through the cooking time. To serve, remove the beef and place on a carving board. Cover with foil and leave to stand for 10–15 minutes to firm up. Cut into slices and transfer to a platter. Spoon over the sauce, garnish with basil and serve immediately.

caribbean beef

ingredients

serves 6

450 g/1 lb braising steak
450 g/1 lb diced pumpkin
    or other squash
1 onion, chopped
1 red pepper, deseeded
    and chopped
2 garlic cloves, finely chopped
2.5-cm/1-inch piece fresh ginger,
    finely chopped
1 tbsp sweet or hot paprika
225 ml/8 fl oz beef stock
400 g/14 oz canned chopped
    tomatoes
400 g/14 oz canned pigeon peas,
    drained and rinsed
400 g/14 oz canned black-eyed
    beans, drained and rinsed

method

1 Preheat the slow cooker, if necessary, or according
to the manufacturer's instructions.

2 Trim off any visible fat from the steak, then dice the
meat. Heat a large, heavy-based saucepan without
adding any extra fat. Add the meat and cook, stirring
constantly, for a few minutes until golden all over. Stir
in the pumpkin, onion, red pepper, garlic and ginger
and cook for 1 minute, then add the paprika, stock and
tomatoes and bring to the boil.

3 Transfer the mixture to the slow cooker, cover and
cook on low for 7 hours. Add the pigeon peas and
black-eyed beans to the stew and season to taste
with salt and pepper. Re-cover and cook on high for
30 minutes, then serve.

beef bourguinon

ingredients

serves 6

6 rashers streaky bacon,
  derinded and chopped
2 tbsp plain flour
900 g/2 lb braising steak,
  trimmed and cut into
  2.5-cm/1-inch cubes
3 tbsp olive oil
25 g/1 oz unsalted butter
12 baby onions or shallots
2 garlic cloves, finely chopped
150 ml/5 fl oz beef stock
450 ml/16 fl oz full-bodied
  red wine
1 bouquet garni
140 g/5 oz mushrooms, sliced
salt and pepper

method

1 Preheat the slow cooker, if necessary, or according to the manufacturer's instructions.

2 Cook the bacon in a large, heavy-based saucepan, stirring occasionally, until the fat runs and the pieces are crisp. Meanwhile, spread out the flour on a plate and season with salt and pepper. Toss the steak cubes in the flour to coat, shaking off any excess. Using a slotted spoon, transfer the bacon to a plate. Add the oil to the saucepan. When it is hot, add the steak cubes and cook, in batches, stirring occasionally, for 5 minutes until browned all over. Transfer to the plate with a slotted spoon.

3 Add the butter to the saucepan. When it has melted, add the onions and garlic and cook, stirring occasionally, for 5 minutes. Return the bacon and steak to the pan and pour in the stock and wine. Bring to the boil.

4 Transfer the mixture to the slow cooker and add the bouquet garni. Cover and cook on low for 7 hours until the meat is tender.

5 Add the mushrooms to the slow cooker and stir well. Re-cover and cook on high for 15 minutes. Remove and discard the bouquet garni. Adjust the seasoning if necessary, then serve immediately.

mediterranean lamb with apricots & pistachio nuts

ingredients

serves 4

1½ tbsp plain flour
1 tsp ground coriander
½ tsp ground cumin
½ tsp ground allspice
450 g/1 lb boneless lamb leg
    steaks, trimmed and cut into
    2.5-cm/1-inch chunks
1 tbsp olive oil
1 onion, chopped
2–3 garlic cloves, chopped
450 ml/16 fl oz lamb or
    chicken stock
pinch of saffron threads, infused
    in 2 tbsp water
1 cinnamon stick
85 g/3 oz dried apricots, chopped
175 g/6 oz courgettes, sliced
115 g/4 oz cherry tomatoes
1 tbsp chopped fresh coriander
salt and pepper
2 tbsp coarsely chopped
    pistachio nuts, to garnish
couscous or rice, to serve

method

1 Preheat the slow cooker, if necessary, or according to the manufacturer's instructions.

2 Mix together the flour, ground coriander, cumin and allspice in a shallow dish, add the lamb and toss until well coated. Reserve the remaining spiced flour.

3 Heat the oil in a heavy-based frying pan. Add the onion and garlic and cook over a low heat, stirring occasionally, for 5 minutes until softened. Add the lamb, increase the heat to high and cook, stirring frequently, for 3 minutes until browned. Sprinkle in the reserved spiced flour and cook, stirring constantly, for 2 minutes, then remove the pan from the heat.

4 Gradually stir in the stock and the saffron with its soaking liquid. Return the pan to the heat and bring to the boil, stirring constantly. Transfer the mixture to the slow cooker and add the cinnamon stick, apricots, courgettes and tomatoes. Cover and cook on low for 8 hours until the meat is tender.

5 Remove and discard the cinnamon stick. Stir in the chopped coriander, season to taste with salt and pepper, sprinkle with the pistachio nuts and serve with couscous or rice.

bouillabaisse

ingredients

serves 6

2.25 kg/5 lb mixed white fish,
  such as red mullet, sea bream,
  sea bass, monkfish and
  whiting, filleted with bones
  and heads reserved, if possible
450 g/1 lb raw prawns, peeled
  and deveined, shells and heads
  reserved, if possible
grated rind of 1 orange
pinch of saffron threads
4 garlic cloves, finely chopped
225 ml/8 fl oz olive oil
2 onions, finely chopped
1 leek, thinly sliced
4 potatoes, thinly sliced
2 large tomatoes,
  peeled and chopped
1 bunch fresh flat-leaf
  parsley, chopped
1 fresh fennel sprig
1 fresh thyme sprig
1 bay leaf
2 cloves
6 black peppercorns
1 strip orange rind
sea salt
crusty bread or croûtes, to serve

method

1 Preheat the slow cooker, if necessary, or according to the manufacturer's instructions.

2 Cut the fish fillets into bite-sized pieces. Place the chunks of fish and the prawns in a large bowl. Sprinkle with the grated orange rind, saffron, half the garlic and 2 tablespoons of the oil. Cover and set aside in the refrigerator.

3 Put the remaining garlic, the onions, leek, potatoes, tomatoes, parsley, fennel, thyme, bay leaf, cloves, peppercorns and strip of orange rind in the slow cooker. Add the fish heads and bones, if using, and the prawn shells and heads. Pour in the remaining olive oil and 2.8 litres/5 pints boiling water or enough to cover the ingredients by 2.5 cm/1 inch. Season with sea salt. Cover and cook on low for 8 hours.

4 Strain the stock and return the liquid to the slow cooker. Discard the flavourings, fish and prawn trimmings but retain the vegetables and return them to the slow cooker if you like. Add the fish and prawn mixture, re-cover and cook on high for 30 minutes until the fish is cooked through and flakes easily.

5 Ladle into warm bowls and serve with crusty bread or croûtes.

moroccan sea bream

ingredients

serves 2

2 tbsp olive oil
2 onions, chopped
2 garlic cloves, finely chopped
2 carrots, finely chopped
1 fennel bulb, finely chopped
½ tsp ground cumin
½ tsp ground cloves
1 tsp ground coriander
pinch of saffron threads
300 ml/10 fl oz fish stock
1 preserved or fresh lemon
900 g/2 lb sea bream, cleaned
salt and pepper

method

1 Preheat the slow cooker, if necessary, or according to the manufacturer's instructions.

2 Heat the oil in a large, heavy-based saucepan. Add the onions, garlic, carrots and fennel and cook over a medium heat, stirring occasionally, for 5 minutes. Stir in all the spices and cook, stirring, for a further 2 minutes. Pour in the stock, season with salt and pepper and bring to the boil.

3 Transfer the mixture to the slow cooker. Cover and cook on low for 6 hours or until the vegetables are tender.

4 Rinse the preserved lemon if using. Discard the fish head if you like. Slice the lemon and place the slices in the fish cavity, then place the fish in the slow cooker. Re-cover and cook on high for 30–45 minutes until the flesh flakes easily.

5 Carefully transfer the fish to a platter and spoon the vegetables around it. Cover and keep warm. Transfer the cooking liquid to a saucepan and boil for a few minutes until reduced. Spoon it over the fish and serve.

vegetable curry

ingredients

serves 4–6

2 tbsp vegetable oil
1 tsp cumin seeds
1 onion, sliced
2 curry leaves
2.5-cm/1-in piece fresh ginger, finely chopped
2 fresh red chillies, deseeded and chopped
2 tbsp curry paste
2 carrots, sliced
115 g/4 oz mangetout
1 cauliflower, cut into florets
3 tomatoes, peeled and chopped
85 g/3 oz frozen peas, thawed
½ tsp turmeric
150–225 ml/5–8 fl oz hot vegetable or chicken stock
salt and pepper

method

1 Preheat the slow cooker, if necessary, or according to the manufacturer's instructions.

2 Heat the oil in a large, heavy-based saucepan. Add the cumin seeds and cook, stirring constantly, for 1–2 minutes until they give off their aroma and begin to pop. Add the onion and curry leaves and cook, stirring occasionally, for 5 minutes until the onion has softened. Add the ginger and chillies and cook, stirring occasionally, for 1 minute.

3 Stir in the curry paste and cook, stirring, for 2 minutes, then add the carrots, mangetout and cauliflower florets. Cook for 5 minutes, then add the tomatoes, peas and turmeric and season with salt and pepper. Cook for 3 minutes, then add 150 ml/5 fl oz of the stock and bring to the boil.

4 Transfer the mixture to the slow cooker. If the vegetables are not covered, add more hot stock, then cover and cook on low for 5 hours until tender. Remove and discard the curry leaves before serving.

variation

For a creamier curry, stir in 125 ml/4 fl oz of coconut milk at the end of cooking and heat through before serving.

vegetable goulash

ingredients

serves 4

15 g/½ oz sun-dried
   tomatoes, chopped
2 tbsp olive oil
½–1 tsp crushed dried chillies
2–3 garlic cloves, chopped
1 large onion, cut into
   small wedges
1 small celeriac, cut into
   small chunks
225 g/8 oz carrots, sliced
225 g/8 oz new potatoes,
   cut into chunks
1 small acorn squash, peeled,
   deseeded and chopped
2 tbsp tomato purée
300 ml/10 fl oz vegetable stock
225 g/8 oz Puy lentils
1–2 tsp hot paprika
3 fresh thyme sprigs,
   plus extra to garnish
450 g/1 lb tomatoes, chopped
soured cream, to serve

method

1 Preheat the slow cooker, if necessary, or according
to the manufacturer's instructions.

2 Put the sun-dried tomatoes in a small heatproof bowl,
add freshly boiled water to cover and leave to soak for
15–20 minutes.

3 Heat the oil in a heavy-based saucepan. Add the
chillies, garlic, onion, celeriac, carrots, potatoes and
squash and cook over a medium–low heat, stirring
frequently, for 5–8 minutes until softened. Mix together
the tomato purée and stock in a jug and stir it into the
pan. Add the lentils, sun-dried tomatoes with their
soaking liquid, the paprika and thyme and bring to
the boil.

4 Transfer the mixture to the slow cooker, cover and cook
on low for 4½ hours. Add the tomatoes, re-cover and
cook on high for 45 minutes until all the vegetables
and lentils are tender. Remove and discard the thyme
sprigs. Serve the goulash topped with soured cream
and garnished with extra thyme sprigs.

moroccan vegetables

ingredients

serves 4

4 tomatoes, peeled,
    deseeded and chopped
700 ml/1¼ pints vegetable stock
1 onion, sliced
2 carrots, diagonally sliced
1 tbsp chopped fresh coriander
175 g/6 oz courgettes, sliced
1 small turnip, cubed
425 g/15 oz canned chickpeas,
    drained and rinsed
½ tsp ground turmeric
¼ tsp ground ginger
¼ tsp ground cinnamon
225 g/8 oz couscous
salt
fresh coriander sprigs, to garnish

method

1 Preheat the slow cooker, if necessary, or according to the manufacturer's instructions.

2 Put half the tomatoes in a blender or food processor and process until smooth. Scrape into a saucepan, add 450 ml/16 fl oz of the stock and bring to the boil. Pour the mixture into the slow cooker, add the remaining tomatoes, the onion, carrots, coriander, courgettes, turnip, chickpeas, turmeric, ginger and cinnamon and stir well. Cover and cook on high for 3 hours.

3 Just before serving, bring the remaining stock to the boil in a large pan. Add a pinch of salt and sprinkle in the couscous, stirring constantly. Remove the pan from the heat, cover and leave to stand for 5 minutes.

4 Fluff up the grains of couscous with a fork and divide it between 4 bowls. Top with the vegetable stew, garnish with coriander sprigs and serve.

sweet & sour sicilian pasta

ingredients

serves 4

4 tbsp olive oil
1 large red onion, sliced
2 garlic cloves, finely chopped
2 red peppers, deseeded and sliced
2 courgettes, cut into batons
1 aubergine, cut into batons
450 ml/16 fl oz passata
4 tbsp lemon juice
2 tbsp balsamic vinegar
55 g/2 oz stoned black olives,
   sliced
1 tbsp sugar
400 g/14 oz dried fettucine
   or pappardelle
salt and pepper
fresh flat-leaf parsley sprigs,
   to garnish

method

1 Preheat the slow cooker, if necessary, or according to the manufacturer's instructions.

2 Heat the oil in a large, heavy-based saucepan. Add the onion, garlic and peppers and cook over a low heat, stirring occasionally, for 5 minutes. Add the courgettes and aubergine and cook, stirring occasionally, for 5 minutes more. Stir in the passata and 150 ml/5 fl oz water and bring to the boil. Stir in the lemon juice, vinegar, olives and sugar and season with salt and pepper.

3 Transfer the mixture to the slow cooker. Cover and cook on low for 5 hours until all the vegetables are tender.

4 To cook the pasta, bring a large saucepan of lightly salted water to the boil. Add the pasta and bring back to the boil. Cook for 10–12 minutes until the pasta is tender but still firm to the bite. Drain and transfer to a warmed serving dish. Spoon the vegetable mixture over the pasta, toss lightly, garnish with parsley and serve.

desserts

chocolate pots

ingredients

serves 6

300 ml/10 fl oz single cream
300 ml/10 fl oz milk
225 g/8 oz plain chocolate,
    broken into small pieces
1 large egg
4 egg yolks
4 tbsp caster sugar
150 ml/5 fl oz double cream
grated chocolate, to decorate

method

1 Preheat the slow cooker, if necessary, or according to the manufacturer's instructions.

2 Pour the single cream and milk into a saucepan and add the chocolate. Set the pan over a very low heat and stir until the chocolate has melted and the mixture is smooth. Remove from the heat and leave to cool for 10 minutes.

3 Beat together the egg, egg yolks and sugar in a bowl until combined. Gradually stir in the chocolate mixture until thoroughly blended, then strain into a jug.

4 Divide the mixture between 6 ramekins and cover with foil. Stand the ramekins on a trivet in the slow cooker and pour in enough boiling water to come about halfway up the sides of the ramekins. Cover and cook on low for 3–3½ hours, until just set. Remove the slow cooker pot from the base and leave to cool completely. Remove the ramekins and chill in the refrigerator for at least 4 hours.

5 Whip the double cream in a bowl until it holds soft peaks. Top each chocolate pot with a little of the whipped cream and decorate with grated chocolate. Serve immediately.

chocolate & walnut sponge

ingredients

serves 4

55 g/2 oz cocoa powder,
  plus extra for dusting
2 tbsp milk
115 g/4 oz self-raising flour
pinch of salt
115 g/4 oz unsalted butter,
  softened, plus extra for
  greasing
115 g/4 oz caster sugar
2 eggs, lightly beaten
55 g/2 oz walnut halves, chopped
whipped cream, to serve

method

1 Preheat the slow cooker, if necessary, or according to the manufacturer's instructions.

2 Grease a 1.2-litre/2-pint pudding basin with butter. Cut out a double round of greaseproof paper that is 7 cm/2¾ inches wider than the rim of the basin. Grease one side with butter and make a pleat in the centre.

3 Mix the cocoa and the milk to a paste in a small bowl. Sift together the flour and salt into a separate small bowl. Set aside.

4 Beat together the butter and sugar in a large bowl until pale and fluffy. Gradually beat in the eggs, a little at a time, then gently fold in the sifted flour mixture, followed by the cocoa mixture and the walnuts.

5 Spoon the mixture into the prepared basin. Cover the basin with the greaseproof paper rounds, buttered-side down, and tie in place with string. Stand the basin on a trivet in the slow cooker and pour in enough boiling water to come about halfway up the side of the basin. Cover and cook on high for 3–3½ hours.

6 Remove the basin from the slow cooker and discard the greaseproof paper. Run a knife around the inside of the basin, then turn out onto a warmed serving dish. Serve with whipped cream, dusted with cocoa.

magic lemon sponge

ingredients

serves 4

140 g/5 oz caster sugar
3 eggs, separated
300 ml/10 fl oz milk
3 tbsp self-raising flour, sifted
150 ml/5 fl oz freshly squeezed
    lemon juice
icing sugar, for dusting

method

1 Preheat the slow cooker, if necessary, or according to the manufacturer's instructions.

2 Beat the sugar with the egg yolks in a bowl, using an electric mixer. Gradually beat in the milk, followed by the flour and the lemon juice.

3 Whisk the egg whites in a separate, grease-free bowl until stiff. Fold half the whites into the yolk mixture using a rubber or plastic spatula in a figure-of-eight movement, then fold in the remainder. Try not to knock out the air.

4 Pour the mixture into an ovenproof dish, cover with foil and place in the slow cooker. Add sufficient boiling water to come about one-third of the way up the side of the dish. Cover and cook on high for 2½ hours until the mixture has set and the sauce and sponge have separated.

5 Lift the dish out of the cooker and discard the foil. Lightly sift a little icing sugar over the top and serve.

italian bread pudding

ingredients

serves 6

unsalted butter, for greasing
6 slices panettone
3 tbsp Marsala
300 ml/10 fl oz milk
300 ml/10 fl oz single cream
100 g/3½ oz caster sugar
grated rind of ½ lemon
pinch of ground cinnamon
3 large eggs, lightly beaten

method

1 Preheat the slow cooker, if necessary, or according to the manufacturer's instructions.

2 Grease a pudding basin and set aside. Place the panettone on a deep plate and sprinkle with the Marsala wine.

3 Pour the milk and cream into a saucepan and add the sugar, lemon rind and cinnamon. Gradually bring to the boil over a low heat, stirring until the sugar has dissolved. Remove the pan from the heat and leave to cool slightly, then pour the mixture onto the eggs, beating constantly.

4 Place the panettone in the prepared dish, pour in the egg mixture and cover with foil. Place in the slow cooker and add enough boiling water to come about one-third of the way up the side of the dish. Cover and cook on high for 2½ hours until set.

5 Remove the dish from the slow cooker and discard the foil. Leave to cool, then chill in the refrigerator until required. Loosen the sides of the pudding and turn out onto a serving dish.

rice pudding

ingredients

serves 4

140 g/5 oz short-grain rice
1 litre/1¾ pints milk
115 g/4 oz sugar
1 tsp vanilla extract
ground cinnamon and 4 cinnamon
    sticks, to decorate

method

1 Preheat the slow cooker, if necessary, or according to the manufacturer's instructions.

2 Rinse the rice well under cold running water and drain thoroughly. Pour the milk into a large, heavy-based saucepan, add the sugar and bring to the boil, stirring constantly. Sprinkle in the rice, stir well and simmer gently for 10–15 minutes. Transfer the mixture to an ovenproof dish and cover with foil.

3 Place the dish in the slow cooker and add boiling water to come about one-third of the way up the side. Cover and cook on high for 2 hours.

4 Remove the dish from the slow cooker and discard the foil. Stir the vanilla extract into the rice, then spoon it into heatproof glasses or bowls. Dust lightly with ground cinnamon and decorate with cinnamon sticks.

variation

For a fruity rice pudding, add 2 tablespoons of crystallized ginger and 2 tablespoons of chopped plumped dried apricots and stir into the pudding before cooking.

thai black rice pudding

ingredients

serves 4

175 g/6 oz black glutinous rice
2 tbsp soft light brown sugar
450 ml/16 fl oz canned
     coconut milk
225 ml/8 fl oz water
3 eggs
2 tbsp caster sugar

method

1 Preheat the slow cooker, if necessary, or according to the manufacturer's instructions.

2 Mix together the rice, brown sugar and half the coconut milk in a saucepan, then stir in the water. Bring to the boil, then reduce the heat and simmer, stirring occasionally, for 15 minutes, until almost all the liquid has been absorbed. Transfer the mixture into individual ovenproof dishes or 1 large dish.

3 Lightly beat the eggs with the remaining coconut milk and the caster sugar. Strain, then pour the mixture over the rice.

4 Cover the dishes with foil. Stand the dish on a trivet in the slow cooker and pour in enough boiling water to come about one third of the way up the sides of the dish. Cover and cook on high for 2–2½ hours, until set. Carefully remove the dishes from the slow cooker and discard the foil. Serve hot or cold.

apple crumble

ingredients

serves 4

55 g/2 oz plain flour
55 g/2 oz rolled oats
150 g/5½ oz light
    muscovado sugar
½ tsp grated nutmeg
½ tsp ground cinnamon
115 g/4 oz butter, softened
4 cooking apples, peeled,
    cored and sliced
4–5 tbsp apple juice
single cream or natural yogurt,
    to serve

method

1 Preheat the slow cooker, if necessary, or according to the manufacturer's instructions.

2 Sift the flour into a bowl and stir in the oats, sugar, nutmeg and cinnamon. Add the butter and mix in with a pastry blender or the prongs of a fork.

3 Place the apple slices in the base of the slow cooker and add the apple juice. Sprinkle the flour mixture evenly over them. Cover and cook on low for 5½ hours.

4 Serve hot, warm or cold, with single cream or yogurt.

blushing pears

ingredients

serves 6

6 small ripe pears
225 ml/8 fl oz ruby port
200 g/7 oz caster sugar
1 tsp finely chopped
    crystallized ginger
2 tbsp lemon juice
whipped cream or Greek yogurt,
    to serve

method

1 Preheat the slow cooker, if necessary, or according to the manufacturer's instructions.

2 Peel the pears, cut them in half lengthways and scoop out the cores. Place them in the slow cooker.

3 Mix together the port, sugar, ginger and lemon juice in a jug and pour the mixture over the pears. Cover and cook on low for 4 hours until the pears are tender.

4 Leave the pears to cool in the slow cooker, then carefully transfer to a bowl, cover and chill in the refrigerator until required.

5 To serve, partially cut each pear half into about 6 slices lengthways, leaving the fruit intact at the stalk end. Carefully lift the pear halves onto serving plates and press gently to fan out the slices. Serve with whipped cream or yogurt.

poached peaches in marsala

ingredients

serves 4-6

150 ml/5 fl oz Marsala
175 ml/6 fl oz water
4 tbsp caster sugar
1 vanilla pod, split lengthways
6 peaches, cut into wedges and
    stoned or 12 apricots,
    halved and stoned
2 tsp cornflour
crème fraîche or Greek yogurt,
    to serve

method

1 Preheat the slow cooker, if necessary, or according to the manufacturer's instructions.

2 Pour the Marsala and 150 ml/5 fl oz of the water into a saucepan and add the sugar and vanilla pod. Set the pan over a low heat and stir until the sugar has dissolved, then bring to the boil without stirring. Remove from the heat.

3 Put the peaches into the slow cooker and pour the syrup over them. Cover and cook on high for 1–1½ hours, until the fruit is tender.

4 Using a slotted spoon, gently transfer the peaches to a serving dish. Remove the vanilla pod from the slow cooker and scrape the seeds into the syrup with the point of a knife. Discard the pod. Stir the cornflour to a paste with the remaining water in a small bowl, then stir into the syrup. Re-cover and cook on high for 15 minutes, stirring occasionally.

5 Spoon the syrup over the fruit and leave to cool slightly. Serve warm or chill in the refrigerator for 2 hours before serving with crème fraîche or yogurt.

crème brûlée

ingredients

serves 6

1 vanilla pod
1 litre/1¾ pints double cream
6 egg yolks
100 g/3½ oz caster sugar
85 g/3 oz soft light brown sugar

method

1 Preheat the slow cooker, if necessary, or according to the manufacturer's instructions.

2 Using a sharp knife, split the vanilla pod in half lengthways, scrape the seeds into a saucepan and add the pod. Pour in the cream and bring just to the boil, stirring constantly. Remove from the heat, cover and leave to infuse for 20 minutes.

3 Whisk together the egg yolks and caster sugar in a bowl until thoroughly mixed. Remove and discard the vanilla pod from the pan, then whisk the cream into the egg yolk mixture. Strain the mixture into a large jug.

4 Divide the mixture between 6 ramekins and cover with foil. Stand the ramekins on a trivet in the slow cooker and pour in enough boiling water to come about halfway up the sides of the ramekins. Cover and cook on low for 3–3½ hours, until just set. Remove the slow cooker pot from the base and leave to cool completely. Remove the ramekins and chill in the refrigerator for at least 4 hours.

5 Preheat the grill. Sprinkle the brown sugar evenly over the surface of each dessert, then cook under the grill for 30–60 seconds, until the sugar has melted and caramelized. Alternatively, you can use a cook's blowtorch. Chill for a further hour before serving.

almond charlotte

ingredients

serves 4

unsalted butter, for greasing
10–12 sponge fingers
300 ml/10 fl oz milk
2 eggs
2 tbsp caster sugar
55 g/2 oz blanched
    almonds, chopped
4–5 drops of almond extract

sherry sauce
1 tbsp caster sugar
3 egg yolks
150 ml/5 fl oz cream sherry

method

1 Preheat the slow cooker, if necessary, or according to the manufacturer's instructions.

2 Grease a 600-ml/1-pint pudding basin with butter. Line the basin with the sponge fingers, cutting them to fit and placing them cut-sides down and sugar-coated sides outwards. Cover the base with some of the offcuts.

3 Pour the milk into a saucepan and bring just to the boil, then remove from the heat. Beat together the eggs and sugar in a heatproof bowl until combined, then stir in the milk. Stir in the almonds and almond extract.

4 Carefully pour the mixture into the prepared basin and cover with foil. Stand the basin on a trivet in the slow cooker and pour in enough boiling water to come about halfway up the side of the dish. Cover and cook on high for 3–3½ hours, until set.

5 To make the sherry sauce, put the sugar, egg yolks and sherry into a heatproof bowl. Set the bowl over a pan of simmering water. Whisk well until the mixture thickens, but do not boil. Remove from the heat.

6 Carefully remove the basin from the slow cooker and discard the foil. Leave to stand for 2–3 minutes, then turn out onto a warmed serving plate. Pour the sherry sauce around it and serve immediately.